The Names *of* God
Bible Promise Book

The Names *of* God
Bible Promise Book

King James Version

BakerBooks

a division of Baker Publishing Group
Grand Rapids, Michigan

Published by Baker Books
a division of Baker Publishing Group
P.O. Box 6287, Grand Rapids, MI 49516-6287
www.bakerbooks.com

Printed in the United States of America

Library of Congress Cataloging-in-Publication Data
Names: Baker Books (Firm)
Title: The KJV names of God Bible promise book.
Description: Grand Rapids, MI : Baker Books, 2016.
Identifiers: LCCN 2015040658 (print) | ISBN 9780801005404
    (imitation leather)
Subjects: LCSH: God—Promises—Biblical teaching. | God—
    Name—Biblical teaching. | Bible—
    Quotations.
Classification: LCC BS680.P68 K55 2016
    (print) | LCC BS680.P68 (ebook) | DDC
    220.5/2036—dc23
LC record available at http://lccn.loc.
    gov/2015040658

Scripture quotations are from the King James Version of the Bible.

In keeping with biblical principles of creation stewardship, Baker Publishing Group advocates the responsible use of our natural resources. As a member of the Green Press Initiative, our company uses recycled paper when possible. The text paper of this book is composed in part of post-consumer waste.

16   17   18   19   20   21   22   7   6   5   4   3   2   1

Contents

Yahweh Elohim:
The Lord God

Yahweh Tsebaoth: *The Lord of Hosts*

God's Promises Offer . . .

God Promises Help When I Feel . . .

Yeshua: *Jesus*

God's Promises Offer . . .

God's Promises Help Me Know . . .

God Promises Help When I Feel . . .

God Promises That I Can Stand Against . . .

Through God's Promises I Experience . . .

Introduction

This pocket-sized book offers a portable reminder of God's many promises of protection, salvation, and guidance with selections of key Scriptures from the beloved KJV translation of the Bible. It is a treasure trove of encouragement for daily challenges that is organized by topic for easy reference. In this special *Names of God Bible Promise Book*, Hebrew transliterations of names and titles of God, such as *Elohim* and *Yahweh*, have been placed within the biblical text to reveal God's names in Bible promises.

Ab

Father

God's Promises Offer . . .

■ *Victory*

A father [Ab] of the fatherless, and a judge of the widows, *is* God [Elohim] in his holy habitation.

God [Elohim] setteth the solitary in families: he bringeth out those which are bound with chains: but the rebellious dwell in a dry *land*.

Psalm 68:5–6

Adonay Yahweh

Lord God

God's Promises Offer . . .

■ *Rescue*

For thus saith the Lord GOD [Adonay Yahweh]; Behold, I, *even* I, will both search my sheep, and seek them out.

As a shepherd seeketh out his flock in the day that he is among his sheep *that are* scattered; so will I seek out my sheep, and will deliver them out of all places where they have been scattered in the cloudy and dark day.

Ezekiel 34:11–12

■ *Strength*

The LORD God [Yahweh Adonay] *is* my strength, and he will make my feet like hinds' *feet*, and he will make me to walk upon mine high places. To the chief singer on my stringed instruments.

Habakkuk 3:19

God Promises Help When I Feel . . .

■ *Worry*

Therefore thus saith the Lord GOD [Adonay Yahweh], Behold, I lay in Zi'-on for a foundation a stone, a tried stone, a precious corner *stone*, a sure foundation: he that believeth shall not make haste.

Isaiah 28:16

God Promises That I Can Stand Against . . .

■ *Death*

He will swallow up death in victory; and the Lord GOD [Adonay Yahweh] will wipe away tears from off all faces; and the rebuke of his people shall he take away from off all the earth: for the LORD [Yahweh] hath spoken *it*.

Isaiah 25:8

El Olam

Everlasting God

God's Promises Offer . . .

■ *Restoration*

Hast thou not known? hast thou not heard, *that* the everlasting God [El Olam], the LORD [Yahweh], the Creator of the ends of the earth, fainteth not, neither is weary? *there is* no searching of his understanding.

He giveth power to the faint; and to *them that have* no might he increaseth strength.

Even the youths shall faint and be weary, and the young men shall utterly fall:

But they that wait upon the LORD [Yahweh] shall renew *their* strength; they shall mount up with wings as eagles; they shall run, and not be weary; *and* they shall walk, and not faint.

Isaiah 40:28–31

Elohim, El, Eloah

God

God's Promises Offer . . .

■ *Comfort*

My flesh and my heart faileth: *but* God [Elohim] *is* the strength of my heart, and my portion for ever.

Psalm 73:26

■ *Consolation*

Surely he hath borne our griefs, and carried our sorrows: yet we did esteem him stricken, smitten of God [Elohim], and afflicted.

Isaiah 53:4

■ *Direction*

It is God [El] that girdeth me with strength, and maketh my way perfect.

Psalm 18:32

■ *Encouragement*

Why art thou cast down, O my soul? and *why* art thou disquieted in me? hope thou in God [Elohim]: for I shall yet praise him *for* the help of his countenance.

Psalm 42:5

■ *Forgiveness*

Who *is* a God [El] like unto thee, that pardoneth iniquity, and passeth by the transgression of the remnant of his heritage? he retaineth not his anger for ever, because he delighteth *in* mercy.

He will turn again, he will have compassion upon us; he will subdue our iniquities; and thou wilt cast all their sins into the depths of the sea.

Micah 7:18–19

■ *Justice*

Thy throne, O God [Elohim], *is* for ever and ever: the sceptre of thy kingdom *is* a right sceptre.

Psalm 45:6

■ *Protection*

Every word of God [Eloah] *is* pure: he *is* a shield [Magen] unto them that put their trust in him.

Proverbs 30:5

■ *Refreshment*

The humble shall see *this*, *and* be glad: and your heart shall live that seek God [Elohim].

For the LORD [Yahweh] heareth the poor, and despiseth not his prisoners.

Psalm 69:32–33

■ *Refuge*

The eternal God [Elohim] *is thy* refuge, and underneath *are* the everlasting arms: and he shall thrust out the enemy from before thee; and shall say, Destroy *them*.

Deuteronomy 33:27

How excellent *is* thy lovingkindness, O God [Elohim]! therefore the children of men put their trust under the shadow of thy wings.

Psalm 36:7

God [Elohim] *is* our refuge [Machseh] and strength, a very present help in trouble.

Psalm 46:1

Trust in him at all times; ye people, pour out your heart before him: God [Elohim] *is* a refuge [Machseh] for us. Se'-lah.

Psalm 62:8

■ *Restoration*

Oh that the salvation of Is'-ra-el *were come* out of Zi'-on! When God [Elohim] bringeth back the captivity of his people, Ja'-cob shall rejoice, *and* Is'-ra-el shall be glad.

Psalm 53:6

■ *Strength*

It is God [El] that girdeth me with strength, and maketh my way perfect.

Psalm 18:32

God [Elohim] *is* our refuge [Machseh] and strength, a very present help in trouble.

Psalm 46:1

Because of his strength will I wait upon thee: for God [Elohim] *is* my defence.

The God [Elohim] of my mercy shall prevent me: God [Elohim] shall let me see *my desire* upon mine enemies.

Psalm 59:9–10

Through God [Elohim] we shall do valiantly: for he *it is that* shall tread down our enemies.

Psalm 60:12

O God [Elohim], *thou art* terrible out of thy holy places: the God [El] of Is'-ra-el *is* he that giveth strength and power unto *his* people. Blessed *be* God [Elohim].

Psalm 68:35

Behold, God [El] *is* my salvation; I will trust, and not be afraid: for the Lord JE-HO'-VAH [Yahweh] *is* my strength and *my* song; he also is become my salvation.

Isaiah 12:2

■ *Success*

Let not mercy and truth forsake thee: bind them about thy neck; write them upon the table of thine heart:

So shalt thou find favour and good understanding in the sight of God [Elohim] and man.

Trust in the LORD [Yahweh] with all thine heart; and lean not unto thine own understanding.

In all thy ways acknowledge him, and he shall direct thy paths.

Proverbs 3:3–6

■ *Victory*

The eternal God [Elohim] *is thy* refuge, and underneath *are* the everlasting arms: and he shall thrust out the enemy from before thee; and shall say, Destroy *them*.

Deuteronomy 33:27

For by thee I have run through a troop: by my God [Elohim] have I leaped over a wall.

Psalm 18:29

When I cry *unto thee*, then shall mine enemies turn back: this I know; for God [Elohim] *is* for me.

Psalm 56:9

Fear thou not; for I *am* with thee: be not dismayed; for I *am* thy God [Elohim]: I will strengthen thee; yea, I will help thee; yea, I will uphold thee with the right hand of my righteousness.

Isaiah 41:10

God's Promises Help Me Know . . .

■ *The Future*

Behold, I will gather them out of all countries, whither I have driven them in mine anger, and in my fury, and in great wrath; and I will bring them again unto this place, and I will cause them to dwell safely:

And they shall be my people, and I will be their God [Elohim]:

And I will give them one heart, and one way, that they may fear me for ever, for the good of them, and of their children after them:

And I will make an everlasting covenant with them, that I will not turn away from them, to do them good; but I will put my fear in their hearts, that they shall not depart from me.

Yea, I will rejoice over them to do them good, and I will plant them in this land assuredly with my whole heart and with my whole soul.

Jeremiah 32:37–41

Moreover I will make a covenant of peace with them; it shall be an everlasting covenant with them: and I will place them, and multiply them, and will set my sanctuary in the midst of them for evermore.

My tabernacle also shall be with them: yea, I will be their God [Elohim], and they shall be my people.

Ezekiel 37:26–27

■ God's Word

The grass withereth, the flower fadeth: but the word of our God [Elohim] shall stand for ever.

Isaiah 40:8

■ Hope for Living

Why art thou cast down, O my soul? and *why* art thou disquieted in me? hope thou in God [Elohim]: for I shall yet praise him *for* the help of his countenance.

Psalm 42:5

My flesh and my heart faileth: *but* God [Elohim] *is* the strength of my heart, and my portion for ever.

Psalm 73:26

Happy *is he* that *hath* the God [El] of Ja'-cob for his help, whose hope *is* in the LORD [Yahweh] his God [Elohim]:
Which made heaven, and earth, the sea, and all that therein *is*: which keepeth truth for ever:

Psalm 146:5–6

And I will sow her unto me in the earth; and I will have mercy upon her that had not obtained mercy; and I will say to *them which were* not my people, Thou *art* my people; and they shall say, *Thou art* my God [Elohim].

Hosea 2:23

■ *Hope for the Resurrection*

For this God [Elohim] *is* our God [Elohim] for ever and ever: he will be our guide *even* unto death.

Psalm 48:14

■ *The Presence of the Father*

There is a river, the streams whereof shall make glad the city of God [Elohim], the holy *place* of the tabernacles of the most High [Elyon].

God [Elohim] *is* in the midst of her; she shall not be moved: God [Elohim] shall help her, *and that* right early.

Psalm 46:4–5

Our God [Elohim] shall come, and shall not keep silence: a fire shall devour before him, and it shall be very tempestuous round about him.

Psalm 50:3

How precious also are thy thoughts unto me, O God [El]! how great is the sum of them!

If I should count them, they are more in number than the sand: when I awake, I am still with thee.

Psalm 139:17–18

Moreover I will make a covenant of peace with them; it shall be an everlasting covenant with them: and I will place them, and multiply them, and will set my sanctuary in the midst of them for evermore.

My tabernacle also shall be with them: yea, I will be their God [Elohim], and they shall be my people.

Ezekiel 37:26–27

God Promises Help When I Feel . . .

■ *Doubt*

Happy *is he* that *hath* the God [El] of Ja'-cob for his help, whose hope *is* in the LORD [Yahweh] his God [Elohim]:

Which made heaven, and earth, the sea, and all that therein *is*: which keepeth truth for ever.

Psalm 146:5–6

God Promises That I Can Stand Against . . .

■ *Death*

For this God [Elohim] *is* our God [Elohim] for ever and ever: he will be our guide *even* unto death.

Psalm 48:14

■ *Persecution*

When I cry *unto thee*, then shall mine enemies turn
back: this I know; for God [Elohim] *is* for me.

Psalm 56:9

■ *Sickness*

My flesh and my heart faileth: *but* God [Elohim] *is* the
strength of my heart, and my portion for ever.

Psalm 73:26

■ *Sin*

Who *is* a God [El] like unto thee, that pardoneth iniquity, and passeth by the transgression of the remnant of
his heritage? he retaineth not his anger for ever, because
he delighteth *in* mercy.

He will turn again, he will have compassion upon us;
he will subdue our iniquities; and thou wilt cast all their
sins into the depths of the sea.

Micah 7:18–19

■ *Suffering*

My flesh and my heart faileth: *but* God [Elohim] *is* the
strength of my heart, and my portion for ever.

Psalm 73:26

Through God's Promises I Experience . . .

■ *Eternal Life*

For this God [Elohim] *is* our God [Elohim] for ever and ever: he will be our guide *even* unto death.

Psalm 48:14

■ *Gifts from God*

And God [Elohim] said, Behold, I have given you every herb bearing seed, which *is* upon the face of all the earth, and every tree, in the which *is* the fruit of a tree yielding seed; to you it shall be for meat.

And to every beast of the earth, and to every fowl of the air, and to every thing that creepeth upon the earth, wherein *there is* life, *I have given* every green herb for meat: and it was so.

Genesis 1:29–30

For thou, O God [Elohim], hast heard my vows: thou hast given *me* the heritage of those that fear thy name.

Psalm 61:5

O God [Elohim], *thou art* terrible out of thy holy places: the God [El] of Is'-ra-el *is* he that giveth strength and power unto *his* people. Blessed *be* God [Elohim].

Psalm 68:35

■ *The Mercy of the Father*

But God [Elohim] will redeem my soul from the power of the grave: for he shall receive me. Se'-lah.

Psalm 49:15

Whoso offereth praise glorifieth me: and to him that ordereth *his* conversation *aright* will I shew the salvation of God [Elohim].

Psalm 50:23

As for me, I will call upon God [Elohim]; and the LORD [Yahweh] shall save me.

Psalm 55:16

Who *is* a God [El] like unto thee, that pardoneth iniquity, and passeth by the transgression of the remnant of his heritage? he retaineth not his anger for ever, because he delighteth *in* mercy.

He will turn again, he will have compassion upon us; he will subdue our iniquities; and thou wilt cast all their sins into the depths of the sea.

Micah 7:18–19

God's Promises Enable My . . .

▪ *Courage*

Fear thou not; for I *am* with thee: be not dismayed; for I *am* thy God [Elohim]: I will strengthen thee; yea, I will help thee; yea, I will uphold thee with the right hand of my righteousness.

Isaiah 41:10

Elyon

Most High

God's Promises Help Me Know . . .

■ *The Presence of the Father*

There is a river, the streams whereof shall make glad the city of God [Elohim], the holy *place* of the tabernacles of the most High [Elyon].

God [Elohim] *is* in the midst of her; she shall not be moved: God [Elohim] shall help her, *and that* right early.

Psalm 46:4–5

God's Promises Offer . . .

■ *Protection*

Because thou hast made the LORD [Yahweh], *which is* my refuge [Machseh], *even* the most High [Elyon], thy habitation;

There shall no evil befall thee, neither shall any plague come nigh thy dwelling.

For he shall give his angels charge over thee, to keep thee in all thy ways.

They shall bear thee up in *their* hands, lest thou dash thy foot against a stone.

Thou shalt tread upon the lion and adder: the young lion and the dragon shalt thou trample under feet.

Because he hath set his love upon me, therefore will I deliver him: I will set him on high, because he hath known my name.

He shall call upon me, and I will answer him: I *will be* with him in trouble; I will deliver him, and honour him.

With long life will I satisfy him, and shew him my salvation.

Psalm 91:9–16

■ *Refuge*

He that dwelleth in the secret place of the most High [Elyon] shall abide under the shadow of the Almighty [Shadday].

Psalm 91:1

Machseh

Refuge

God's Promises Offer . . .

■ *Protection*

Because thou hast made the LORD [Yahweh], *which is* my refuge [Machseh], *even* the most High [Elyon], thy habitation;

There shall no evil befall thee, neither shall any plague come nigh thy dwelling.

For he shall give his angels charge over thee, to keep thee in all thy ways.

They shall bear thee up in *their* hands, lest thou dash thy foot against a stone.

Thou shalt tread upon the lion and adder: the young lion and the dragon shalt thou trample under feet.

Because he hath set his love upon me, therefore will I deliver him: I will set him on high, because he hath known my name.

He shall call upon me, and I will answer him: I *will be* with him in trouble; I will deliver him, and honour him.

With long life will I satisfy him, and shew him my salvation.

Psalm 91:9–16

▣ *Refuge*

God [Elohim] *is* our refuge [Machseh] and strength, a very present help in trouble.

Psalm 46:1

Trust in him at all times; ye people, pour out your heart before him: God [Elohim] *is* a refuge [Machseh] for us. Se'-lah.

Psalm 62:8

▣ *Strength*

From the end of the earth will I cry unto thee, when my heart is overwhelmed: lead me to the rock *that* is higher than I.

For thou hast been a shelter [Machseh] for me, *and* a strong tower [Migdal-Oz] from the enemy.

Psalm 61:2–3

Magen

Shield

God's Promises Offer . . .

■ *Joy*

The LORD [Yahweh] *is* my strength and my shield [Magen]; my heart trusted in him, and I am helped: therefore my heart greatly rejoiceth; and with my song will I praise him.

Psalm 28:7

Our soul waiteth for the LORD [Yahweh]: he *is* our help and our shield [Magen].

For our heart shall rejoice in him, because we have trusted in his holy name.

Psalm 33:20–21

■ *Protection*

Ye that fear the LORD [Yahweh], trust in the LORD [Yahweh]: he *is* their help and their shield [Magen].

Psalm 115:11

Every word of God [Eloah] *is* pure: he *is* a shield [Magen] unto them that put their trust in him.

Proverbs 30:5

Through God's Promises I Experience . . .

■ *Gifts from God*

For the LORD God [Yahweh Elohim] *is* a sun and shield [Magen]: the LORD [Yahweh] will give grace and glory: no good *thing* will he withhold from them that walk uprightly.

Psalm 84:11

For the LORD [Yahweh] giveth wisdom: out of his mouth *cometh* knowledge and understanding.

He layeth up sound wisdom for the righteous: *he is* a buckler [Magen] to them that walk uprightly.

He keepeth the paths of judgment, and preserveth the way of his saints.

Proverbs 2:6–8

Ruach

Spirit

God's Promises Help Me Know . . .

■ *The Presence of the Holy Spirit*

And it shall come to pass afterward, *that* I will pour out my spirit [Ruach] upon all flesh; and your sons and your daughters shall prophesy, your old men shall dream dreams, your young men shall see visions:

And also upon the servants and upon the handmaids in those days will I pour out my spirit [Ruach].

And I will shew wonders in the heavens and in the earth, blood, and fire, and pillars of smoke.

The sun shall be turned into darkness, and the moon into blood, before the great and terrible day of the LORD [Yahweh] come.

And it shall come to pass, *that* whosoever shall call on the name of the LORD [Yahweh] shall be delivered: for in mount Zi'-on and in Je-ru'-sa-lem shall be deliverance, as the LORD [Yahweh] hath said, and in the remnant whom the LORD [Yahweh] shall call.

Joel 2:28–32

God's Promises Enable My . . .

■ *Obedience*

A new heart also will I give you, and a new spirit will I put within you: and I will take away the stony heart out of your flesh, and I will give you an heart of flesh.

And I will put my spirit [Ruach] within you, and cause you to walk in my statutes, and ye shall keep my judgments, and do *them*.

And ye shall dwell in the land that I gave to your fathers; and ye shall be my people, and I will be your God [Elohim].

Ezekiel 36:26–28

■ *Wisdom*

And there shall come forth a rod out of the stem of Jes'-se, and a Branch shall grow out of his roots:

And the spirit of the LORD [Ruach Yahweh] shall rest upon him, the spirit [Ruach] of wisdom and understanding, the spirit [Ruach] of counsel and might, the spirit [Ruach] of knowledge and of the fear of the LORD [Yahweh].

Isaiah 11:1–2

God's Promises Guide Me In . . .

▩ *Humility*

The Spir'-it [Ruach] of the Lord GOD [Adonay Yahweh] *is* upon me; because the LORD [Yahweh] hath anointed me to preach good tidings unto the meek; he hath sent me to bind up the brokenhearted, to proclaim liberty to the captives, and the opening of the prison to *them that are* bound;

To proclaim the acceptable year of the LORD [Yahweh], and the day of vengeance of our God [Elohim]; to comfort all that mourn;

To appoint unto them that mourn in Zi'-on, to give unto them beauty for ashes, the oil of joy for mourning, the garment of praise for the spirit of heaviness; that they might be called trees of righteousness, the planting of the LORD [Yahweh], that he might be glorified.

Isaiah 61:1–3

Sar Shalom

The Prince of Peace

God's Promises Offer . . .

■ *Peace*

For unto us a child is born, unto us a son is given: and the government shall be upon his shoulder: and his name shall be called Wonderful, Counsellor, The mighty God, The everlasting Father, The Prince of Peace [Sar Shalom].

Of the increase of *his* government and peace *there shall be* no end, upon the throne of Da'-vid, and upon his kingdom, to order it, and to establish it with judgment and with justice from henceforth even for ever. The zeal of the LORD of hosts [Yahweh Tsebaoth] will perform this.

Isaiah 9:6–7

Yahweh, Yah

The Lord

God's Promises Offer . . .

▨ *Comfort*

Blessed *is* he that considereth the poor: the LORD [Yahweh] will deliver him in time of trouble.

The LORD [Yahweh] will preserve him, and keep him alive; *and* he shall be blessed upon the earth: and thou wilt not deliver him unto the will of his enemies.

The LORD [Yahweh] will strengthen him upon the bed of languishing: thou wilt make all his bed in his sickness.

Psalm 41:1–3

Sing, O heavens; and be joyful, O earth; and break forth into singing, O mountains: for the LORD [Yahweh] hath comforted his people, and will have mercy upon his afflicted.

Isaiah 49:13

■ Consolation

The LORD [Yahweh] *is* nigh unto them that are of a broken heart; and saveth such as be of a contrite spirit.

Psalm 34:18

And the ransomed of the LORD [Yahweh] shall return, and come to Zi'-on with songs and everlasting joy upon their heads: they shall obtain joy and gladness, and sorrow and sighing shall flee away.

Isaiah 35:10

■ Direction

The LORD [Yahweh] *is* the portion of mine inheritance and of my cup: thou maintainest my lot.

The lines are fallen unto me in pleasant *places*; yea, I have a goodly heritage.

Psalm 16:5–6

If thou, LORD [Yah], shouldst mark iniquities, O Lord [Adonay], who shall stand?

But *there is* forgiveness with thee, that thou mayest be feared.

Psalm 130:3–4

But this *shall be* the covenant that I will make with the house of Is'-ra-el; After those days, saith the LORD [Yahweh], I will put my law in their inward parts, and write it in their hearts; and will be their God [Elohim], and they shall be my people.

And they shall teach no more every man his neighbour, and every man his brother, saying, Know the LORD [Yahweh]: for they shall all know me, from the least of them unto the greatest of them, saith the LORD [Yahweh]: for I will forgive their iniquity, and I will remember their sin no more.

Jeremiah 31:33–34

And rend your heart, and not your garments, and turn unto the LORD [Yahweh] your God [Elohim]: for he *is* gracious and merciful, slow to anger, and of great kindness, and repenteth him of the evil.

Joel 2:13

Rejoice not against me, O mine enemy: when I fall, I shall arise; when I sit in darkness, the LORD [Yahweh] *shall be* a light unto me.

I will bear the indignation of the LORD [Yahweh], because I have sinned against him, until he plead my cause, and execute judgment for me: he will bring me forth to the light, *and* I shall behold his righteousness.

Micah 7:8–9

■ *Healing*

Blessed *is* he that considereth the poor: the LORD [Yahweh] will deliver him in time of trouble.

The LORD [Yahweh] will preserve him, and keep him alive; *and* he shall be blessed upon the earth: and thou wilt not deliver him unto the will of his enemies.

The LORD [Yahweh] will strengthen him upon the bed of languishing: thou wilt make all his bed in his sickness.

Psalm 41:1–3

Come, and let us return unto the LORD [Yahweh]: for he hath torn, and he will heal us; he hath smitten, and he will bind us up.

After two days will he revive us: in the third day he will raise us up, and we shall live in his sight.

Then shall we know, *if* we follow on to know the LORD [Yahweh]: his going forth is prepared as the morning; and he shall come unto us as the rain, as the latter *and* former rain unto the earth.

Hosea 6:1–3

■ Joy

The LORD [Yahweh] *is* my strength and my shield [Magen]; my heart trusted in him, and I am helped: therefore my heart greatly rejoiceth; and with my song will I praise him.

Psalm 28:7

Our soul waiteth for the LORD [Yahweh]: he *is* our help and our shield [Magen].

For our heart shall rejoice in him, because we have trusted in his holy name.

Psalm 33:20–21

Then was our mouth filled with laughter, and our tongue with singing: then said they among the heathen, The LORD [Yahweh] hath done great things for them.

Psalm 126:2

And the ransomed of the LORD [Yahweh] shall return, and come to Zi'-on with songs and everlasting joy upon their heads: they shall obtain joy and gladness, and sorrow and sighing shall flee away.

Isaiah 35:10

Sing, O heavens; and be joyful, O earth; and break forth into singing, O mountains: for the LORD [Yahweh] hath comforted his people, and will have mercy upon his afflicted.

Isaiah 49:13

Break forth into joy, sing together, ye waste places of Je-ru'-sa-lem: for the LORD [Yahweh] hath comforted his people, he hath redeemed Je-ru'-sa-lem.

The LORD [Yahweh] hath made bare his holy arm in the eyes of all the nations; and all the ends of the earth shall see the salvation of our God [Elohim].

Isaiah 52:9–10

If thou turn away thy foot from the sabbath, *from* doing thy pleasure on my holy day; and call the sabbath a delight, the holy of the LORD [Yahweh], honourable; and shalt honour him, not doing thine own ways, nor finding thine own pleasure, nor speaking *thine own* words:

Then shalt thou delight thyself in the LORD [Yahweh]; and I will cause thee to ride upon the high places of the earth, and feed thee with the heritage of Ja'-cob thy father: for the mouth of the LORD [Yahweh] hath spoken *it*.

Isaiah 58:13–14

I will greatly rejoice in the LORD [Yahweh], my soul shall be joyful in my God [Elohim]; for he hath clothed me with the garments of salvation, he hath covered me with the robe of righteousness, as a bridegroom decketh *himself* with ornaments, and as a bride adorneth *herself* with her jewels.

Isaiah 61:10

■ *Justice*

The LORD [Yahweh] will not leave him in his hand, nor condemn him when he is judged.

Psalm 37:33

Which executeth judgment for the oppressed: which giveth food to the hungry. The LORD [Yahweh] looseth the prisoners.

Psalm 146:7

And shall make him of quick understanding in the fear of the LORD [Yahweh]: and he shall not judge after the sight of his eyes, neither reprove after the hearing of his ears:

But with righteousness shall he judge the poor, and reprove with equity for the meek of the earth: and he shall smite the earth with the rod of his mouth, and with the breath of his lips shall he slay the wicked.

And righteousness shall be the girdle of his loins, and faithfulness the girdle of his reins.

Isaiah 11:3–5

■ *Peace*

The LORD [Yahweh] will give strength unto his people; the LORD [Yahweh] will bless his people with peace.

Psalm 29:11

Blessed *is* the man whom thou chastenest, O LORD [Yah], and teachest him out of thy law;

That thou mayest give him rest from the days of adversity, until the pit be digged for the wicked.

Psalm 94:12–13

When a man's ways please the LORD [Yahweh], he maketh even his enemies to be at peace with him.

Proverbs 16:7

For the mountains shall depart, and the hills be removed; but my kindness shall not depart from thee, neither shall the covenant of my peace be removed, saith the LORD [Yahweh] that hath mercy on thee.

Isaiah 54:10

And all thy children *shall be* taught of the LORD [Yahweh]; and great *shall be* the peace of thy children.

Isaiah 54:13

Neither let the son of the stranger, that hath joined himself to the LORD [Yahweh], speak, saying, The LORD [Yahweh] hath utterly separated me from his people: neither let the eunuch say, Behold, I *am* a dry tree.

Isaiah 56:3

And of Ben'-ja-min he said, The beloved of the LORD [Yahweh] shall dwell in safety by him; *and the* LORD [Yahweh] shall cover him all the day long, and he shall dwell between his shoulders.

Deuteronomy 33:12

For the oppression of the poor, for the sighing of the needy, now will I arise, saith the LORD [Yahweh]; I will set *him* in safety *from him that* puffeth at him.

The words of the LORD [Yahweh] *are* pure words: *as* silver tried in a furnace of earth, purified seven times.

Psalm 12:5–6

The LORD [Yahweh] *is* my light and my salvation; whom shall I fear? the LORD [Yahweh] *is* the strength of my life; of whom shall I be afraid?

Psalm 27:1

Many *are* the afflictions of the righteous: but the LORD [Yahweh] delivereth him out of them all.

He keepeth all his bones: not one of them is broken.

Psalm 34:19–20

The steps of a *good* man are ordered by the LORD [Yahweh]: and he delighteth in his way.

Though he fall, he shall not be utterly cast down: for the LORD [Yahweh] upholdeth *him with* his hand.

I have been young, and *now* am old; yet have I not seen the righteous forsaken, nor his seed begging bread. *He is* ever merciful, and lendeth; and his seed *is* blessed.

Psalm 37:23–26

For the LORD [Yahweh] loveth judgment, and forsaketh not his saints; they are preserved for ever: but the seed of the wicked shall be cut off.

Psalm 37:28

Cast thy burden upon the LORD [Yahweh], and he shall sustain thee: he shall never suffer the righteous to be moved.

Psalm 55:22

Because thou hast made the LORD [Yahweh], *which is* my refuge [Machseh], *even* the most High [Elyon], thy habitation;

There shall no evil befall thee, neither shall any plague come nigh thy dwelling.

For he shall give his angels charge over thee, to keep thee in all thy ways.

They shall bear thee up in *their* hands, lest thou dash thy foot against a stone.

Thou shalt tread upon the lion and adder: the young lion and the dragon shalt thou trample under feet.

Because he hath set his love upon me, therefore will I deliver him: I will set him on high, because he hath known my name.

He shall call upon me, and I will answer him: I *will be* with him in trouble; I will deliver him, and honour him.

With long life will I satisfy him, and shew him my salvation.

Psalm 91:9–16

Ye that fear the LORD [Yahweh], trust in the LORD [Yahweh]: he *is* their help and their shield [Magen].

Psalm 115:11

Which executeth judgment for the oppressed: which giveth food to the hungry. The LORD [Yahweh] looseth the prisoners:

The LORD [Yahweh] openeth *the eyes of* the blind: the LORD [Yahweh] raiseth them that are bowed down: the LORD [Yahweh] loveth the righteous:

The LORD [Yahweh] preserveth the strangers; he relieveth the fatherless and widow: but the way of the wicked he turneth upside down.

Psalm 146:7–9

The name of the LORD [Yahweh] *is* a strong tower [Migdal-Oz]: the righteous runneth into it, and is safe.

Proverbs 18:10

But now thus saith the LORD [Yahweh] that created thee, O Ja'-cob, and he that formed thee, O Is'-ra-el, Fear not: for I have redeemed thee, I have called *thee* by thy name; thou *art* mine.

When thou passest through the waters, I *will be* with thee; and through the rivers, they shall not overflow thee: when thou walkest through the fire, thou shalt not be burned; neither shall the flame kindle upon thee.

Isaiah 43:1–2

■ *Provision*

Surely goodness and mercy shall follow me all the days of my life: and I will dwell in the house of the Lord [Yahweh] for ever.

Psalm 23:6

O fear the Lord [Yahweh], ye his saints: for *there is* no want to them that fear him.
The young lions do lack, and suffer hunger: but they that seek the Lord [Yahweh] shall not want any good *thing*.

Psalm 34:9–10

Yea, the Lord [Yahweh] shall give *that which is* good; and our land shall yield her increase.
Righteousness shall go before him; and shall set *us* in the way of his steps.

Psalm 85:12–13

■ *Refreshment*

The LORD [Yahweh] *is* my shepherd [Roeh]; I shall not want.

He maketh me to lie down in green pastures: he leadeth me beside the still waters.

He restoreth my soul: he leadeth me in the paths of righteousness for his name's sake.

Psalm 23:1–3

■ *Refuge*

The LORD [Yahweh] *is* my light and my salvation; whom shall I fear? the LORD [Yahweh] *is* the strength of my life; of whom shall I be afraid?

Psalm 27:1

O taste and see that the LORD [Yahweh] *is* good: blessed *is* the man *that* trusteth in him.

Psalm 34:8

The LORD [Yahweh] redeemeth the soul of his servants: and none of them that trust in him shall be desolate.

Psalm 34:22

Because thou hast made the LORD [Yahweh], *which is* my refuge [Machseh], *even* the most High [Elyon], thy habitation;

There shall no evil befall thee, neither shall any plague come nigh thy dwelling.

For he shall give his angels charge over thee, to keep thee in all thy ways.

They shall bear thee up in *their* hands, lest thou dash thy foot against a stone.

Thou shalt tread upon the lion and adder: the young lion and the dragon shalt thou trample under feet.

Psalm 91:9–13

The Lord [Yahweh] *is* good, a strong hold in the day of trouble; and he knoweth them that trust in him.

Nahum 1:7

■ *Rescue*

The angel of the Lord [Yahweh] encampeth round about them that fear him, and delivereth them.

Psalm 34:7

The righteous cry, and the Lord [Yahweh] heareth, and delivereth them out of all their troubles.

Psalm 34:17

Many *are* the afflictions of the righteous: but the Lord [Yahweh] delivereth him out of them all.

He keepeth all his bones: not one of them is broken.

Psalm 34:19–20

But the salvation of the righteous *is* of the Lord [Yahweh]: *he is* their strength in the time of trouble.

And the LORD [Yahweh] shall help them, and deliver them: he shall deliver them from the wicked, and save them, because they trust in him.

Psalm 37:39–40

I waited patiently for the LORD [Yahweh]; and he inclined unto me, and heard my cry.

He brought me up also out of an horrible pit, out of the miry clay, and set my feet upon a rock, *and* established my goings.

And he hath put a new song in my mouth, *even* praise unto our God [Elohim]: many shall see *it*, and fear, and shall trust in the LORD [Yahweh].

Psalm 40:1–3

Let Is'-ra-el hope in the LORD [Yahweh]: for with the LORD [Yahweh] *there is* mercy, and with him *is* plenteous redemption.

And he shall redeem Is'-ra-el from all his iniquities.

Psalm 130:7–8

And I will restore to you the years that the locust hath eaten, the cankerworm, and the caterpiller, and the palmerworm, my great army which I sent among you.

And ye shall eat in plenty, and be satisfied, and praise the name of the LORD [Yahweh] your God [Elohim], that hath dealt wondrously with you: and my people shall never be ashamed.

And ye shall know that I *am* in the midst of Is'-ra-el, and *that* I *am* the LORD [Yahweh] your God [Elohim], and none else: and my people shall never be ashamed.

Joel 2:25–27

■ *Rest*

I will lift up mine eyes unto the hills, from whence cometh my help.

My help *cometh* from the LORD [Yahweh], which made heaven and earth.

He will not suffer thy foot to be moved: he that keepeth thee will not slumber.

Behold, he that keepeth Is'-ra-el shall neither slumber nor sleep.

The LORD [Yahweh] *is* thy keeper: the LORD [Yahweh] *is* thy shade upon thy right hand.

The sun shall not smite thee by day, nor the moon by night.

The LORD [Yahweh] shall preserve thee from all evil: he shall preserve thy soul.

The LORD [Yahweh] shall preserve thy going out and thy coming in from this time forth, and even for evermore.

Psalm 121

■ Restoration

Thus saith the LORD [Yahweh], In an acceptable time have I heard thee, and in a day of salvation have I helped thee: and I will preserve thee, and give thee for a covenant of the people, to establish the earth, to cause to inherit the desolate heritages.

Isaiah 49:8

■ Security

But the LORD [Yahweh] shall endure for ever: he hath prepared his throne for judgment.

And he shall judge the world in righteousness, he shall minister judgment to the people in uprightness.

The LORD [Yahweh] also will be a refuge for the oppressed, a refuge in times of trouble.

And they that know thy name will put their trust in thee: for thou, LORD [Yahweh], hast not forsaken them that seek thee.

Psalm 9:7–10

The LORD [Yahweh] *is* my shepherd [Roeh]; I shall not want.

Psalm 23:1

■ *Strength*

The LORD [Yahweh] *is* my strength and my shield [Magen]; my heart trusted in him, and I am helped: therefore my heart greatly rejoiceth; and with my song will I praise him.

The LORD [Yahweh] *is* their strength, and he *is* the saving strength of his anointed.

Psalm 28:7–8

The LORD [Yahweh] will give strength unto his people; the LORD [Yahweh] will bless his people with peace.

Psalm 29:11

The name of the LORD [Yahweh] *is* a strong tower [Migdal-Oz]: the righteous runneth into it, and is safe.

Proverbs 18:10

He giveth power to the faint; and to *them that have* no might he increaseth strength.

Even the youths shall faint and be weary, and the young men shall utterly fall:

But they that wait upon the LORD [Yahweh] shall renew *their* strength; they shall mount up with wings as eagles; they shall run, and not be weary; *and* they shall walk, and not faint.

Isaiah 40:29–31

And the LORD [Yahweh] shall guide thee continually, and satisfy thy soul in drought, and make fat thy bones: and thou shalt be like a watered garden, and like a spring of water, whose waters fail not.

Isaiah 58:11

■ *Success*

Commit thy works unto the LORD [Yahweh], and thy thoughts shall be established.

Proverbs 16:3

He that handleth a matter wisely shall find good: and whoso trusteth in the LORD [Yahweh], happy *is* he.

Proverbs 16:20

By humility *and* the fear of the LORD [Yahweh] *are* riches, and honour, and life.

Proverbs 22:4

Then he answered and spake unto me, saying, This *is* the word of the LORD [Yahweh] unto Ze-rub'-ba-bel, saying, Not by might, nor by power, but by my spirit [Ruach], saith the LORD of hosts [Yahweh Tsebaoth].

Zechariah 4:6

■ *Victory*

Some *trust* in chariots, and some in horses: but we will remember the name of the Lord [Yahweh] our God [Elohim].

They are brought down and fallen: but we are risen, and stand upright.

Psalm 20:7–8

The Lord [Yahweh] *is* my strength and my shield [Magen]; my heart trusted in him, and I am helped: therefore my heart greatly rejoiceth; and with my song will I praise him.

Psalm 28:7

The Lord [Yahweh] upholdeth all that fall, and raiseth up all *those that be* bowed down.

Psalm 145:14

Be not afraid of sudden fear, neither of the desolation of the wicked, when it cometh.

For the Lord [Yahweh] shall be thy confidence, and shall keep thy foot from being taken.

Proverbs 3:25–26

Blessed *is* the man that trusteth in the Lord [Yahweh], and whose hope the Lord [Yahweh] is.

Jeremiah 17:7

God's Promises Help Me Know . . .

▥ *The Future*

Our soul waiteth for the LORD [Yahweh]: he *is* our help and our shield [Magen].

For our heart shall rejoice in him, because we have trusted in his holy name.

Psalm 33:20–21

Wait on the LORD [Yahweh], and keep his way, and he shall exalt thee to inherit the land: when the wicked are cut off, thou shalt see *it*.

Psalm 37:34

I will lift up mine eyes unto the hills, from whence cometh my help.

My help *cometh* from the LORD [Yahweh], which made heaven and earth.

He will not suffer thy foot to be moved: he that keepeth thee will not slumber.

Behold, he that keepeth Is'-ra-el shall neither slumber nor sleep.

The LORD [Yahweh] *is* thy keeper: the LORD [Yahweh] *is* thy shade upon thy right hand.

The sun shall not smite thee by day, nor the moon by night.

The LORD [Yahweh] shall preserve thee from all evil: he shall preserve thy soul.

The LORD [Yahweh] shall preserve thy going out and thy coming in from this time forth, and even for evermore.

Psalm 121

Let Is'-ra-el hope in the LORD [Yahweh]: for with the LORD [Yahweh] *there is* mercy, and with him *is* plenteous redemption.

And he shall redeem Is'-ra-el from all his iniquities.

Psalm 130:7–8

Trust in the LORD [Yahweh] with all thine heart; and lean not unto thine own understanding.

In all thy ways acknowledge him, and he shall direct thy paths.

Proverbs 3:5–6

Be not afraid of sudden fear, neither of the desolation of the wicked, when it cometh.

For the LORD [Yahweh] shall be thy confidence, and shall keep thy foot from being taken.

Proverbs 3:25–26

But they that wait upon the LORD [Yahweh] shall renew *their* strength; they shall mount up with wings as eagles; they shall run, and not be weary; *and* they shall walk, and not faint.

Isaiah 40:31

But now thus saith the LORD [Yahweh] that created thee, O Ja'-cob, and he that formed thee, O Is'-ra-el, Fear not: for I have redeemed thee, I have called *thee* by thy name; thou *art* mine.

When thou passest through the waters, I *will be* with thee; and through the rivers, they shall not overflow thee: when thou walkest through the fire, thou shalt not be burned; neither shall the flame kindle upon thee.

Isaiah 43:1–2

For I know the thoughts that I think toward you, saith the LORD [Yahweh], thoughts of peace, and not of evil, to give you an expected end.

Then shall ye call upon me, and ye shall go and pray unto me, and I will hearken unto you.

And ye shall seek me, and find *me*, when ye shall search for me with all your heart.

Jeremiah 29:11–13

■ God's Word

For ever, O LORD [Yahweh], thy word is settled in heaven.

Psalm 119:89

▪ *Hope for Eternal Life*

Surely goodness and mercy shall follow me all the days of my life: and I will dwell in the house of the LORD [Yahweh] for ever.

Psalm 23:6

▪ *Hope for Living*

Wait on the LORD [Yahweh]: be of good courage, and he shall strengthen thine heart: wait, I say, on the LORD [Yahweh].

Psalm 27:14

For the LORD [Yahweh] *is* good; his mercy *is* everlasting; and his truth *endureth* to all generations.

Psalm 100:5

Praise ye the LORD. O give thanks unto the LORD [Yahweh]; for *he is* good: for his mercy *endureth* for ever.

Psalm 106:1

O praise the LORD [Yahweh], all ye nations: praise him, all ye people.

For his merciful kindness is great toward us: and the truth of the LORD [Yahweh] *endureth* for ever. Praise ye the LORD.

Psalm 117

The Lord [Yahweh] shall preserve thy going out and thy coming in from this time forth, and even for evermore.

Psalm 121:8

But they that wait upon the Lord [Yahweh] shall renew *their* strength; they shall mount up with wings as eagles; they shall run, and not be weary; *and* they shall walk, and not faint.

Isaiah 40:31

For ye shall go out with joy, and be led forth with peace: the mountains and the hills shall break forth before you into singing, and all the trees of the field shall clap *their* hands.

Instead of the thorn shall come up the fir tree, and instead of the brier shall come up the myrtle tree: and it shall be to the Lord [Yahweh] for a name, for an everlasting sign *that* shall not be cut off.

Isaiah 55:12–13

This I recall to my mind, therefore have I hope.

It is of the Lord's [Yahweh's] mercies that we are not consumed, because his compassions fail not.

They are new every morning: great *is* thy faithfulness.

The Lord [Yahweh] *is* my portion, saith my soul; therefore will I hope in him.

The Lord [Yahweh] *is* good unto them that wait for him, to the soul *that* seeketh him.

Lamentations 3:21–25

■ *Hope for the Resurrection*

Precious in the sight of the LORD [Yahweh] *is* the death of his saints.

Psalm 116:15

■ *The Presence of the Father*

Thou shalt not be affrighted at them: for the LORD [Yahweh] thy God [Elohim] *is* among you, a mighty God [El] and terrible.

Deuteronomy 7:21

Be strong and of a good courage, fear not, nor be afraid of them: for the LORD [Yahweh] thy God [Elohim], he *it is* that doth go with thee; he will not fail thee, nor forsake thee.

Deuteronomy 31:6

Have not I commanded thee? Be strong and of a good courage; be not afraid, neither be thou dismayed: for the LORD [Yahweh] thy God [Elohim] *is* with thee whithersoever thou goest.

Joshua 1:9

Ye shall not *need* to fight in this *battle*: set yourselves, stand ye *still*, and see the salvation of the LORD [Yahweh] with you, O Ju'-dah and Je-ru'-sa-lem: fear not, nor be dismayed; to morrow go out against them: for the LORD [Yahweh] *will be* with you.

2 Chronicles 20:17

The angel of the LORD [Yahweh] encampeth round about them that fear him, and delivereth them.

Psalm 34:7

The eyes of the LORD [Yahweh] *are* upon the righteous, and his ears *are open* unto their cry.

Psalm 34:15

The righteous cry, and the LORD [Yahweh] heareth, and delivereth them out of all their troubles.

Psalm 34:17

The LORD [Yahweh] *is* nigh unto them that are of a broken heart; and saveth such as be of a contrite spirit.

Psalm 34:18

For in thee, O LORD [Yahweh], do I hope: thou wilt hear, O Lord [Adonay] my God [Elohim].

Psalm 38:15

For I know the thoughts that I think toward you, saith the LORD [Yahweh], thoughts of peace, and not of evil, to give you an expected end.

Then shall ye call upon me, and ye shall go and pray unto me, and I will hearken unto you.

And ye shall seek me, and find *me*, when ye shall search for me with all your heart.

Jeremiah 29:11–13

Come, and let us return unto the LORD [Yahweh]: for he hath torn, and he will heal us; he hath smitten, and he will bind us up.

After two days will he revive us: in the third day he will raise us up, and we shall live in his sight.

Then shall we know, *if* we follow on to know the LORD [Yahweh]: his going forth is prepared as the morning; and he shall come unto us as the rain, as the latter *and* former rain unto the earth.

Hosea 6:1–3

Sow to yourselves in righteousness, reap in mercy; break up your fallow ground: for *it is* time to seek the LORD [Yahweh], till he come and rain righteousness upon you.

Hosea 10:12

In that day it shall be said to Je-ru'-sa-lem, Fear thou not: *and to* Zi'-on, Let not thine hands be slack.

The LORD [Yahweh] thy God [Elohim] in the midst of thee *is* mighty; he will save, he will rejoice over thee with joy; he will rest in his love, he will joy over thee with singing.

Zephaniah 3:16–17

■ *The Presence of the Holy Spirit*

Then he answered and spake unto me, saying, This *is* the word of the LORD [Yahweh] unto Ze-rub'-ba-bel, saying, Not by might, nor by power, but by my spirit [Ruach], saith the LORD of hosts [Yahweh Tsebaoth].

Zechariah 4:6

God Promises Help When I Feel . . .

■ *Anger*

Cease from anger, and forsake wrath: fret not thyself in any wise to do evil.

For evildoers shall be cut off: but those that wait upon the LORD [Yahweh], they shall inherit the earth.

Psalm 37:8–9

■ *Confusion*

Trust in the LORD [Yahweh] with all thine heart; and lean not unto thine own understanding.

In all thy ways acknowledge him, and he shall direct thy paths.

Proverbs 3:5–6

■ Discouragement

When my father and my mother forsake me, then the
LORD [Yahweh] will take me up.

Psalm 27:10

I will greatly praise the LORD [Yahweh] with my mouth;
yea, I will praise him among the multitude.

For he shall stand at the right hand of the poor, to save
him from those that condemn his soul.

Psalm 109:30–31

■ Dissatisfaction

But the LORD [Yahweh] shall endure for ever: he hath
prepared his throne for judgment.

And he shall judge the world in righteousness, he shall
minister judgment to the people in uprightness.

The LORD [Yahweh] also will be a refuge for the oppressed, a refuge in times of trouble.

And they that know thy name will put their trust in
thee: for thou, LORD [Yahweh], hast not forsaken them
that seek thee.

Psalm 9:7–10

The fear of the LORD [Yahweh] *is* clean, enduring for
ever: the judgments of the LORD [Yahweh] *are* true *and*
righteous altogether.

More to be desired *are they* than gold, yea, than much
fine gold: sweeter also than honey and the honeycomb.

Moreover by them is thy servant warned: *and* in keeping of them *there is* great reward.

Psalm 19:9–11

Say among the heathen *that* the LORD [Yahweh] reigneth: the world also shall be established that it shall not be moved: he shall judge the people righteously.

Psalm 96:10

The LORD [Yahweh] executeth righteousness and judgment for all that are oppressed.

Psalm 103:6

The LORD [Yahweh] *is* righteous in all his ways, and holy in all his works.

Psalm 145:17

■ *Doubt*

Be strong and of a good courage, fear not, nor be afraid of them: for the LORD [Yahweh] thy God [Elohim], he *it is* that doth go with thee; he will not fail thee, nor forsake thee.

Deuteronomy 31:6

Because I will publish the name of the LORD [Yahweh]: ascribe ye greatness unto our God [Elohim].

He is the Rock, his work *is* perfect: for all his ways *are* judgment: a God [El] of truth and without iniquity, just and right *is* he.

Deuteronomy 32:3–4

The LORD [Yahweh] *is* the portion of mine inheritance and of my cup: thou maintainest my lot.

The lines are fallen unto me in pleasant *places*; yea, I have a goodly heritage.

Psalm 16:5–6

For the LORD [Yahweh] *is* good; his mercy *is* everlasting; and his truth *endureth* to all generations.

Psalm 100:5

O praise the LORD [Yahweh], all ye nations: praise him, all ye people.

For his merciful kindness is great toward us: and the truth of the LORD [Yahweh] *endureth* for ever. Praise ye the LORD.

Psalm 117

The LORD [Yahweh] *is* righteous in all his ways, and holy in all his works.

Psalm 145:17

For the mountains shall depart, and the hills be removed; but my kindness shall not depart from thee, neither shall the covenant of my peace be removed, saith the LORD [Yahweh] that hath mercy on thee.

Isaiah 54:10

This I recall to my mind, therefore have I hope.

It is of the LORD's [Yahweh's] mercies that we are not consumed, because his compassions fail not.

They are new every morning: great *is* thy faithfulness.

The LORD [Yahweh] *is* my portion, saith my soul; therefore will I hope in him.

The LORD [Yahweh] *is* good unto them that wait for him, to the soul *that* seeketh him.

Lamentations 3:21–25

▨ *Fear*

Thou shalt not be affrighted at them: for the LORD [Yahweh] thy God [Elohim] *is* among you, a mighty God [El] and terrible.

Deuteronomy 7:21

The LORD [Yahweh] *is* my light and my salvation; whom shall I fear? the LORD [Yahweh] *is* the strength of my life; of whom shall I be afraid?

Psalm 27:1

But now thus saith the LORD [Yahweh] that created thee, O Ja'-cob, and he that formed thee, O Is'-ra-el, Fear not: for I have redeemed thee, I have called *thee* by thy name; thou *art* mine.

When thou passest through the waters, I *will be* with thee; and through the rivers, they shall not overflow thee: when thou walkest through the fire, thou shalt not be burned; neither shall the flame kindle upon thee.

Isaiah 43:1–2

■ *Loneliness*

Be strong and of a good courage, fear not, nor be afraid of them: for the LORD [Yahweh] thy God [Elohim], he *it is* that doth go with thee; he will not fail thee, nor forsake thee.

Deuteronomy 31:6

When my father and my mother forsake me, then the LORD [Yahweh] will take me up.

Psalm 27:10

The LORD [Yahweh] *is* nigh unto them that are of a broken heart; and saveth such as be of a contrite spirit.

Psalm 34:18

■ *Weariness*

And the LORD [Yahweh] shall guide thee continually, and satisfy thy soul in drought, and make fat thy bones: and thou shalt be like a watered garden, and like a spring of water, whose waters fail not.

Isaiah 58:11

■ *Worry*

Thou shalt not be affrighted at them: for the LORD [Yahweh] thy God [Elohim] *is* among you, a mighty God [El] and terrible.

Deuteronomy 7:21

Break forth into joy, sing together, ye waste places of Je-ru'-sa-lem: for the LORD [Yahweh] hath comforted his people, he hath redeemed Je-ru'-sa-lem.

The LORD [Yahweh] hath made bare his holy arm in the eyes of all the nations; and all the ends of the earth shall see the salvation of our God [Elohim].

Isaiah 52:9–10

God Promises That I Can Stand Against . . .

■ *Death*

Precious in the sight of the LORD [Yahweh] *is* the death of his saints.

Psalm 116:15

■ *Depression*

The LORD [Yahweh] *is* nigh unto them that are of a broken heart; and saveth such as be of a contrite spirit.

Psalm 34:18

I waited patiently for the LORD [Yahweh]; and he inclined unto me, and heard my cry.

He brought me up also out of an horrible pit, out of the miry clay, and set my feet upon a rock, *and* established my goings.

And he hath put a new song in my mouth, *even* praise unto our God [Elohim]: many shall see *it*, and fear, and shall trust in the LORD [Yahweh].

Psalm 40:1–3

■ *Failure*

The LORD [Yahweh] *is* gracious, and full of compassion; slow to anger, and of great mercy.

Psalm 145:8

And rend your heart, and not your garments, and turn unto the LORD [Yahweh] your God [Elohim]: for he *is* gracious and merciful, slow to anger, and of great kindness, and repenteth him of the evil.

Joel 2:13

■ *Sickness*

Blessed *is* he that considereth the poor: the LORD [Yahweh] will deliver him in time of trouble.

The LORD [Yahweh] will preserve him, and keep him alive; *and* he shall be blessed upon the earth: and thou wilt not deliver him unto the will of his enemies.

The Lord [Yahweh] will strengthen him upon the bed of languishing: thou wilt make all his bed in his sickness.

Psalm 41:1–3

■ *Sin*

Let Is'-ra-el hope in the Lord [Yahweh]: for with the Lord [Yahweh] *there is* mercy, and with him *is* plenteous redemption.

And he shall redeem Is'-ra-el from all his iniquities.

Psalm 130:7–8

Come now, and let us reason together, saith the Lord [Yahweh]: though your sins be as scarlet, they shall be as white as snow; though they be red like crimson, they shall be as wool.

Isaiah 1:18

But this *shall be* the covenant that I will make with the house of Is'-ra-el; After those days, saith the Lord [Yahweh], I will put my law in their inward parts, and write it in their hearts; and will be their God [Elohim], and they shall be my people.

And they shall teach no more every man his neighbour, and every man his brother, saying, Know the Lord [Yahweh]: for they shall all know me, from the least of them unto the greatest of them, saith the Lord [Yahweh]: for I will forgive their iniquity, and I will remember their sin no more.

Jeremiah 31:33–34

■ *Suffering*

For the oppression of the poor, for the sighing of the needy, now will I arise, saith the LORD [Yahweh]; I will set *him* in safety *from him that* puffeth at him.

The words of the LORD [Yahweh] *are* pure words: *as* silver tried in a furnace of earth, purified seven times.

Psalm 12:5–6

Blessed *is* he that considereth the poor: the LORD [Yahweh] will deliver him in time of trouble.

The LORD [Yahweh] will preserve him, and keep him alive; *and* he shall be blessed upon the earth: and thou wilt not deliver him unto the will of his enemies.

The LORD [Yahweh] will strengthen him upon the bed of languishing: thou wilt make all his bed in his sickness.

Psalm 41:1–3

Through God's Promises I Experience . . .

■ *Eternal Life*

Surely goodness and mercy shall follow me all the days of my life: and I will dwell in the house of the LORD [Yahweh] for ever.

Psalm 23:6

The LORD [Yahweh] *is* the portion of mine inheritance and of my cup: thou maintainest my lot.

The lines are fallen unto me in pleasant *places*; yea, I have a goodly heritage.

Psalm 16:5–6

The LORD [Yahweh] *is* my strength and my shield [Magen]; my heart trusted in him, and I am helped: therefore my heart greatly rejoiceth; and with my song will I praise him.

Psalm 28:7

The LORD [Yahweh] will give strength unto his people; the LORD [Yahweh] will bless his people with peace.

Psalm 29:11

Blessed *is* the man whom thou chastenest, O LORD [Yah], and teachest him out of thy law;

That thou mayest give him rest from the days of adversity, until the pit be digged for the wicked.

Psalm 94:12–13

But the mercy of the LORD [Yahweh] *is* from everlasting to everlasting upon them that fear him, and his righteousness unto children's children.

Psalm 103:17

Lo, children *are* an heritage of the LORD [Yahweh]: *and* the fruit of the womb *is his* reward.

As arrows *are* in the hand of a mighty man, so *are* children of the youth.

Happy *is* the man that hath his quiver full of them: they shall not be ashamed, but they shall speak with the enemies in the gate.

Psalm 127:3–5

The LORD [Yahweh] hath sworn *in* truth unto Da'-vid; he will not turn from it; Of the fruit of thy body will I set upon thy throne.

If thy children will keep my covenant and my testimony that I shall teach them, their children shall also sit upon thy throne for evermore.

Psalm 132:11–12

For the LORD [Yahweh] giveth wisdom: out of his mouth *cometh* knowledge and understanding.

He layeth up sound wisdom for the righteous: *he is* a buckler [Magen] to them that walk uprightly.

He keepeth the paths of judgment, and preserveth the way of his saints.

Proverbs 2:6–8

By humility *and* the fear of the LORD [Yahweh] *are* riches, and honour, and life.

Proverbs 22:4

He giveth power to the faint; and to *them that have* no might he increaseth strength.

Even the youths shall faint and be weary, and the young men shall utterly fall:

But they that wait upon the LORD [Yahweh] shall renew *their* strength; they shall mount up with wings as eagles; they shall run, and not be weary; *and* they shall walk, and not faint.

Isaiah 40:29–31

As for me, this *is* my covenant with them, saith the LORD [Yahweh]; My spirit [Ruach] that *is* upon thee, and my words which I have put in thy mouth, shall not depart out of thy mouth, nor out of the mouth of thy seed, nor out of the mouth of thy seed's seed, saith the LORD [Yahweh], from henceforth and for ever.

Isaiah 59:21

But this *shall be* the covenant that I will make with the house of Is'-ra-el; After those days, saith the LORD [Yahweh], I will put my law in their inward parts, and write it in their hearts; and will be their God [Elohim], and they shall be my people.

And they shall teach no more every man his neighbour, and every man his brother, saying, Know the LORD [Yahweh]: for they shall all know me, from the least of them unto the greatest of them, saith the LORD [Yahweh]: for I will forgive their iniquity, and I will remember their sin no more.

Jeremiah 31:33–34

▪ Marriage as God Intended

Whoso findeth a wife findeth a good *thing*, and obtaineth favour of the LORD [Yahweh].

Proverbs 18:22

▪ The Mercy of the Father

Cast thy burden upon the LORD [Yahweh], and he shall sustain thee: he shall never suffer the righteous to be moved.

Psalm 55:22

Mercy and truth are met together; righteousness and peace have kissed *each other*.

Truth shall spring out of the earth; and righteousness shall look down from heaven.

Yea, the LORD [Yahweh] shall give *that which is* good; and our land shall yield her increase.

Righteousness shall go before him; and shall set *us* in the way of his steps.

Psalm 85:10–13

The LORD [Yahweh] *is* merciful and gracious, slow to anger, and plenteous in mercy.

Psalm 103:8

But the mercy of the LORD [Yahweh] *is* from everlasting to everlasting upon them that fear him, and his righteousness unto children's children;

To such as keep his covenant, and to those that remember his commandments to do them.

Psalm 103:17–18

Who *is* like unto the LORD [Yahweh] our God [Elo-
him], who dwelleth on high,

Who humbleth *himself* to behold *the things that are*
in heaven, and in the earth!

He raiseth up the poor out of the dust, *and* lifteth the
needy out of the dunghill;

That he may set *him* with princes, *even* with the princes
of his people.

He maketh the barren woman to keep house, *and to
be* a joyful mother of children. Praise ye the LORD.

Psalm 113:5–9

He will bless them that fear the LORD [Yahweh], *both*
small and great.

Psalm 115:13

Let Is'-ra-el hope in the LORD [Yahweh]: for with the
LORD [Yahweh] *there is* mercy, and with him *is* plenteous
redemption.

And he shall redeem Is'-ra-el from all his iniquities.

Psalm 130:7–8

The LORD [Yahweh] *is* gracious, and full of compassion; slow to anger, and of great mercy.

Psalm 145:8

And rend your heart, and not your garments, and turn unto the LORD [Yahweh] your God [Elohim]: for he *is* gracious and merciful, slow to anger, and of great kindness, and repenteth him of the evil.

Joel 2:13

■ *Opportunities*

All the paths of the LORD [Yahweh] *are* mercy and truth unto such as keep his covenant and his testimonies.

Psalm 25:10

The steps of a *good* man are ordered by the LORD [Yahweh]: and he delighteth in his way.

Though he fall, he shall not be utterly cast down: for the LORD [Yahweh] upholdeth *him with* his hand.

Psalm 37:23–24

Wait on the LORD [Yahweh], and keep his way, and he shall exalt thee to inherit the land: when the wicked are cut off, thou shalt see *it*.

Psalm 37:34

Trust in the LORD [Yahweh] with all thine heart; and lean not unto thine own understanding.

In all thy ways acknowledge him, and he shall direct thy paths.

Proverbs 3:5–6

He that handleth a matter wisely shall find good: and whoso trusteth in the LORD [Yahweh], happy *is* he.

Proverbs 16:20

And *if* thou draw out thy soul to the hungry, and satisfy the afflicted soul; then shall thy light rise in obscurity, and thy darkness *be* as the noon day:

And the LORD [Yahweh] shall guide thee continually, and satisfy thy soul in drought, and make fat thy bones: and thou shalt be like a watered garden, and like a spring of water, whose waters fail not.

And *they that shall be* of thee shall build the old waste places: thou shalt raise up the foundations of many generations; and thou shalt be called, The repairer of the breach, The restorer of paths to dwell in.

Isaiah 58:10–12

God's Promises Enable My . . .

■ *Belief*

He that handleth a matter wisely shall find good: and whoso trusteth in the LORD [Yahweh], happy *is* he.

Proverbs 16:20

Be strong and of a good courage, fear not, nor be afraid of them: for the LORD [Yahweh] thy God [Elohim], he *it is* that doth go with thee; he will not fail thee, nor forsake thee.

Deuteronomy 31:6

Have not I commanded thee? Be strong and of a good courage; be not afraid, neither be thou dismayed: for the LORD [Yahweh] thy God [Elohim] *is* with thee whithersoever thou goest.

Joshua 1:9

Ye shall not *need* to fight in this *battle*: set yourselves, stand ye *still*, and see the salvation of the LORD [Yahweh] with you, O Ju'-dah and Je-ru'-sa-lem: fear not, nor be dismayed; to morrow go out against them: for the LORD [Yahweh] *will be* with you.

2 Chronicles 20:17

Wait on the LORD [Yahweh]: be of good courage, and he shall strengthen thine heart: wait, I say, on the LORD [Yahweh].

Psalm 27:14

Be not afraid of sudden fear, neither of the desolation of the wicked, when it cometh.

For the LORD [Yahweh] shall be thy confidence, and shall keep thy foot from being taken.

Proverbs 3:25–26

Blessed *is* the man that trusteth in the LORD [Yahweh], and whose hope the LORD [Yahweh] is.

Jeremiah 17:7

In that day it shall be said to Je-ru′-sa-lem, Fear thou not: *and to* Zi′-on, Let not thine hands be slack.

The LORD [Yahweh] thy God [Elohim] in the midst of thee *is* mighty; he will save, he will rejoice over thee with joy; he will rest in his love, he will joy over thee with singing.

Zephaniah 3:16–17

■ *Endurance*

Let not thine heart envy sinners: but *be thou* in the fear of the LORD [Yahweh] all the day long.

For surely there is an end; and thine expectation shall not be cut off.

Proverbs 23:17–18

■ *Patience*

I waited patiently for the LORD [Yahweh]; and he inclined unto me, and heard my cry.

He brought me up also out of an horrible pit, out of the miry clay, and set my feet upon a rock, *and* established my goings.

And he hath put a new song in my mouth, *even* praise unto our God [Elohim]: many shall see *it*, and fear, and shall trust in the Lord [Yahweh].

Psalm 40:1–3

The Lord [Yahweh] *is* merciful and gracious, slow to anger, and plenteous in mercy.

Psalm 103:8

The Lord [Yahweh] *is* gracious, and full of compassion; slow to anger, and of great mercy.

Psalm 145:8

And rend your heart, and not your garments, and turn unto the Lord [Yahweh] your God [Elohim]: for he *is* gracious and merciful, slow to anger, and of great kindness, and repenteth him of the evil.

Joel 2:13

■ *Perseverance*

Let not thine heart envy sinners: but *be thou* in the fear of the Lord [Yahweh] all the day long.

For surely there is an end; and thine expectation shall not be cut off.

Proverbs 23:17–18

■ *Trust*

Our soul waiteth for the Lord [Yahweh]: he *is* our help and our shield [Magen].

For our heart shall rejoice in him, because we have trusted in his holy name.

Psalm 33:20–21

It is better to trust in the Lord [Yahweh] than to put confidence in man.

Psalm 118:8

Trust in the Lord [Yahweh] with all thine heart; and lean not unto thine own understanding.

In all thy ways acknowledge him, and he shall direct thy paths.

Proverbs 3:5–6

He that handleth a matter wisely shall find good: and whoso trusteth in the Lord [Yahweh], happy *is* he.

Proverbs 16:20

Trust ye in the Lord [Yahweh] for ever: for in the Lord JE-HO′-VAH [Yah Yahweh] *is* everlasting strength.

Isaiah 26:4

God's Promises Guide Me In . . .

■ *Change*

The counsel of the LORD [Yahweh] standeth for ever, the thoughts of his heart to all generations.

Psalm 33:11

Say among the heathen *that* the LORD [Yahweh] reigneth: the world also shall be established that it shall not be moved: he shall judge the people righteously.

Psalm 96:10

For the mountains shall depart, and the hills be removed; but my kindness shall not depart from thee, neither shall the covenant of my peace be removed, saith the LORD [Yahweh] that hath mercy on thee.

Isaiah 54:10

Neither let the son of the stranger, that hath joined himself to the LORD [Yahweh], speak, saying, The LORD [Yahweh] hath utterly separated me from his people: neither let the eunuch say, Behold, I *am* a dry tree.

Isaiah 56:3

For I *am* the LORD [Yahweh], I change not; therefore ye sons of Ja'-cob are not consumed.

Malachi 3:6

▩ *Decisions*

Trust in the LORD [Yahweh] with all thine heart; and lean not unto thine own understanding.

In all thy ways acknowledge him, and he shall direct thy paths.

Proverbs 3:5–6

▩ *Fear of the Lord*

The angel of the LORD [Yahweh] encampeth round about them that fear him, and delivereth them.

Psalm 34:7

But the mercy of the LORD [Yahweh] *is* from everlasting to everlasting upon them that fear him, and his righteousness unto children's children.

Psalm 103:17

Ye that fear the LORD [Yahweh], trust in the LORD [Yahweh]: he *is* their help and their shield [Magen].

Psalm 115:11

He will bless them that fear the LORD [Yahweh], *both* small and great.

Psalm 115:13

If thou, LORD [Yah], shouldst mark iniquities, O Lord [Adonay], who shall stand?

But *there is* forgiveness with thee, that thou mayest be feared.

Psalm 130:3–4

By humility *and* the fear of the LORD [Yahweh] *are* riches, and honour, and life.

Proverbs 22:4

Let not thine heart envy sinners: but *be thou* in the fear of the LORD [Yahweh] all the day long.

For surely there is an end; and thine expectation shall not be cut off.

Proverbs 23:17–18

■ Giving to God

Because I will publish the name of the LORD [Yahweh]: ascribe ye greatness unto our God [Elohim].

He is the Rock, his work *is* perfect: for all his ways *are* judgment: a God [El] of truth and without iniquity, just and right *is* he.

Deuteronomy 32:3–4

■ Honesty

Who shall ascend into the hill of the LORD [Yahweh]? or who shall stand in his holy place?

He that hath clean hands, and a pure heart; who hath not lifted up his soul unto vanity, nor sworn deceitfully.

He shall receive the blessing from the LORD [Yahweh], and righteousness from the God [Elohim] of his salvation.

Psalm 24:3–5

◼ *Humility*

The LORD [Yahweh] *is* nigh unto them that are of a broken heart; and saveth such as be of a contrite spirit.

Psalm 34:18

By humility *and* the fear of the LORD [Yahweh] *are* riches, and honour, and life.

Proverbs 22:4

And shall make him of quick understanding in the fear of the LORD [Yahweh]: and he shall not judge after the sight of his eyes, neither reprove after the hearing of his ears:

But with righteousness shall he judge the poor, and reprove with equity for the meek of the earth: and he shall smite the earth with the rod of his mouth, and with the breath of his lips shall he slay the wicked.

And righteousness shall be the girdle of his loins, and faithfulness the girdle of his reins.

Isaiah 11:3–5

Sing, O heavens; and be joyful, O earth; and break forth into singing, O mountains: for the LORD [Yahweh] hath comforted his people, and will have mercy upon his afflicted.

Isaiah 49:13

For all those *things* hath mine hand made, and all those *things* have been, saith the LORD [Yahweh]: but to this *man* will I look, *even* to *him that is* poor and of a contrite spirit, and trembleth at my word.

Isaiah 66:2

■ *Money*

O fear the LORD [Yahweh], ye his saints: for *there is* no want to them that fear him.

The young lions do lack, and suffer hunger: but they that seek the LORD [Yahweh] shall not want any good *thing*.

Psalm 34:9–10

Yea, the LORD [Yahweh] shall give *that which is* good; and our land shall yield her increase.

Righteousness shall go before him; and shall set *us* in the way of his steps.

Psalm 85:12–13

■ Prayer

When the LORD [Yahweh] shall build up Zi'-on, he shall appear in his glory.

He will regard the prayer of the destitute, and not despise their prayer.

Psalm 102:16–17

The LORD [Yahweh] *is* nigh unto all them that call upon him, to all that call upon him in truth.

Psalm 145:18

Therefore I will look unto the LORD [Yahweh]; I will wait for the God [Elohim] of my salvation; my God [Elohim] will hear me.

Micah 7:7

■ Purpose

For I know the thoughts that I think toward you, saith the LORD [Yahweh], thoughts of peace, and not of evil, to give you an expected end.

Then shall ye call upon me, and ye shall go and pray unto me, and I will hearken unto you.

And ye shall seek me, and find *me*, when ye shall search for me with all your heart.

Jeremiah 29:11–13

For then will I turn to the people a pure language, that they may all call upon the name of the LORD [Yahweh], to serve him with one consent.

Zephaniah 3:9

▧ Wisdom

Talk no more so exceeding proudly; let *not* arrogancy come out of your mouth: for the LORD [Yahweh] *is* a God [El] of knowledge, and by him actions are weighed.

1 Samuel 2:3

Thy righteousness *is* like the great mountains; thy judgments *are* a great deep: O LORD [Yahweh], thou preservest man and beast.

Psalm 36:6

For the LORD [Yahweh] giveth wisdom: out of his mouth *cometh* knowledge and understanding.

He layeth up sound wisdom for the righteous: *he is* a buckler [Magen] to them that walk uprightly.

He keepeth the paths of judgment, and preserveth the way of his saints.

Proverbs 2:6–8

■ *Work*

Commit thy works unto the LORD [Yahweh], and thy
thoughts shall be established.

Proverbs 16:3

■ *Worship*

Because I will publish the name of the LORD [Yahweh]:
ascribe ye greatness unto our God [Elohim].

He is the Rock, his work *is* perfect: for all his ways
are judgment: a God [El] of truth and without iniquity,
just and right *is* he.

Deuteronomy 32:3–4

Thou, *even* thou, *art* LORD [Yahweh] alone; thou hast
made heaven, the heaven of heavens, with all their host,
the earth, and all *things* that *are* therein, the seas, and
all that *is* therein, and thou preservest them all; and the
host of heaven worshippeth thee.

Nehemiah 9:6

The LORD [Yahweh] *is* my strength and my shield
[Magen]; my heart trusted in him, and I am helped:
therefore my heart greatly rejoiceth; and with my song
will I praise him.

The LORD [Yahweh] *is* their strength, and he *is* the
saving strength of his anointed.

Psalm 28:7–8

I waited patiently for the LORD [Yahweh]; and he inclined unto me, and heard my cry.

He brought me up also out of an horrible pit, out of the miry clay, and set my feet upon a rock, *and* established my goings.

And he hath put a new song in my mouth, *even* praise unto our God [Elohim]: many shall see *it*, and fear, and shall trust in the LORD [Yahweh].

Psalm 40:1–3

O come, let us worship and bow down: let us kneel before the LORD [Yahweh] our maker.

For he *is* our God [Elohim]; and we *are* the people of his pasture, and the sheep of his hand. To day if ye will hear his voice.

Psalm 95:6–7

The LORD [Yahweh] reigneth; let the earth rejoice; let the multitude of isles be glad *thereof*.

Psalm 97:1

Praise ye the LORD. O give thanks unto the LORD [Yahweh]; for *he is* good: for his mercy *endureth* for ever.

Psalm 106:1

I will greatly praise the LORD [Yahweh] with my mouth; yea, I will praise him among the multitude.

For he shall stand at the right hand of the poor, to save *him* from those that condemn his soul.

Psalm 109:30–31

O praise the LORD [Yahweh], all ye nations: praise him, all ye people.

For his merciful kindness is great toward us: and the truth of the LORD [Yahweh] *endureth* for ever. Praise ye the LORD.

Psalm 117

If thou turn away thy foot from the sabbath, *from* doing thy pleasure on my holy day; and call the sabbath a delight, the holy of the LORD [Yahweh], honourable; and shalt honour him, not doing thine own ways, nor finding thine own pleasure, nor speaking *thine own* words:

Then shalt thou delight thyself in the LORD [Yahweh]; and I will cause thee to ride upon the high places of the earth, and feed thee with the heritage of Ja'-cob thy father: for the mouth of the LORD [Yahweh] hath spoken *it*.

Isaiah 58:13–14

I will greatly rejoice in the LORD [Yahweh], my soul shall be joyful in my God [Elohim]; for he hath clothed me with the garments of salvation, he hath covered me with the robe of righteousness, as a bridegroom decketh *himself* with ornaments, and as a bride adorneth *herself* with her jewels.

Isaiah 61:10

For then will I turn to the people a pure language, that they may all call upon the name of the LORD [Yahweh], to serve him with one consent.

Zephaniah 3:9

Yahweh Elohim

The Lord God

Through God's Promises I Experience . . .

■ *Gifts from God*

For the LORD God [Yahweh Elohim] *is* a sun and shield [Magen]: the LORD [Yahweh] will give grace and glory: no good *thing* will he withhold from them that walk uprightly.

Psalm 84:11

■ *Marriage as God Intended*

And the LORD God [Yahweh Elohim] said, *It is* not good that the man should be alone; I will make him an help meet for him. . . .

Therefore shall a man leave his father and his mother, and shall cleave unto his wife: and they shall be one flesh.

Genesis 2:18, 24

Yahweh Tsebaoth

The Lord of Hosts

God's Promises Offer . . .

■ *Peace*

For unto us a child is born, unto us a son is given: and the government shall be upon his shoulder: and his name shall be called Wonderful, Counsellor, The mighty God, The everlasting Father, The Prince of Peace [Sar Shalom].

Of the increase of *his* government and peace *there shall be* no end, upon the throne of Da'-vid, and upon his kingdom, to order it, and to establish it with judgment and with justice from henceforth even for ever. The zeal of the LORD of hosts [Yahweh Tsebaoth] will perform this.

Isaiah 9:6–7

■ *Success*

Then he answered and spake unto me, saying, This *is* the word of the LORD [Yahweh] unto Ze-rub'-ba-bel, saying, Not by might, nor by power, but by my spirit [Ruach], saith the LORD of hosts [Yahweh Tsebaoth].

Zechariah 4:6

God Promises Help When I Feel . . .

■ *Fear*

The LORD of hosts [Yahweh Tsebaoth] *is* with us; the God [Elohim] of Ja'-cob *is* our refuge. Se'-lah.

Psalm 46:7

Yeshua

Jesus

God's Promises Offer . . .

■ *Comfort*

Blessed *be* God, even the Father of our Lord Je'-sus [Yeshua] Christ, the Father of mercies, and the God of all comfort;

Who comforteth us in all our tribulation, that we may be able to comfort them which are in any trouble, by the comfort wherewith we ourselves are comforted of God.

For as the sufferings of Christ abound in us, so our consolation also aboundeth by Christ.

2 Corinthians 1:3–5

For God hath not appointed us to wrath, but to obtain salvation by our Lord Je'-sus [Yeshua] Christ,

Who died for us, that, whether we wake or sleep, we should live together with him.

Wherefore comfort yourselves together, and edify one another, even as also ye do.

1 Thessalonians 5:9–11

Now our Lord Je'-sus [Yeshua] Christ himself, and God, even our Father, which hath loved us, and hath given *us* everlasting consolation and good hope through grace,

Comfort your hearts, and stablish you in every good word and work.

2 Thessalonians 2:16–17

For men verily swear by the greater: and an oath for confirmation *is* to them an end of all strife.

Wherein God, willing more abundantly to shew unto the heirs of promise the immutability of his counsel, confirmed *it* by an oath:

That by two immutable things, in which *it was* impossible for God to lie, we might have a strong consolation, who have fled for refuge to lay hold upon the hope set before us:

Which *hope* we have as an anchor of the soul, both sure and stedfast, and which entereth into that within the veil;

Whither the forerunner is for us entered, *even* Je'-sus [Yeshua], made an high priest for ever after the order of Mel-chis'-e-dec.

Hebrews 6:16–20

■ *Forgiveness*

And as they were eating, Je'-sus [Yeshua] took bread, and blessed *it*, and brake *it*, and gave *it* to the disciples, and said, Take, eat; this is my body.

And he took the cup, and gave thanks, and gave *it* to them, saying, Drink ye all of it;

For this is my blood of the new testament, which is shed for many for the remission of sins.

Matthew 26:26–28

Then Pe'-ter said unto them, Repent, and be baptized every one of you in the name of Je'-sus [Yeshua] Christ for the remission of sins, and ye shall receive the gift of the Ho'-ly Ghost.

For the promise is unto you, and to your children, and to all that are afar off, *even* as many as the Lord our God shall call.

Acts 2:38–39

There is therefore now no condemnation to them which are in Christ Je'-sus [Yeshua], who walk not after the flesh, but after the Spir'-it.

For the law of the Spir'-it of life in Christ Je'-sus [Ye-shua] hath made me free from the law of sin and death.

Romans 8:1–2

But if we walk in the light, as he is in the light, we have fellowship one with another, and the blood of Je'-sus [Yeshua] Christ his Son cleanseth us from all sin.

1 John 1:7

■ *Growth*

Now therefore ye are no more strangers and foreigners, but fellowcitizens with the saints, and of the household of God;

And are built upon the foundation of the apostles and prophets, Je'-sus [Yeshua] Christ himself being the chief corner *stone*;

In whom all the building fitly framed together groweth unto an holy temple in the Lord:

In whom ye also are builded together for an habitation of God through the Spir'-it.

Ephesians 2:19–22

Being filled with the fruits of righteousness, which are by Je'-sus [Yeshua] Christ, unto the glory and praise of God.

Philippians 1:11

As newborn babes, desire the sincere milk of the word, that ye may grow thereby:

If so be ye have tasted that the Lord *is* gracious.

To whom coming, *as unto* a living stone, disallowed indeed of men, but chosen of God, *and* precious,

Ye also, as lively stones, are built up a spiritual house, an holy priesthood, to offer up spiritual sacrifices, acceptable to God by Je'-sus [Yeshua] Christ.

Wherefore also it is contained in the scripture, Behold, I lay in Si'-on a chief corner stone, elect, precious: and he that believeth on him shall not be confounded.

1 Peter 2:2–6

■ *Joy*

Rejoice in the Lord alway: *and* again I say, Rejoice.

Let your moderation be known unto all men. The Lord *is* at hand.

Be careful for nothing; but in every thing by prayer and supplication with thanksgiving let your requests be made known unto God.

And the peace of God, which passeth all understanding, shall keep your hearts and minds through Christ Je'-sus [Yeshua].

Philippians 4:4–7

That which was from the beginning, which we have heard, which we have seen with our eyes, which we have looked upon, and our hands have handled, of the Word of life;

(For the life was manifested, and we have seen *it*, and bear witness, and shew unto you that eternal life, which was with the Father, and was manifested unto us;)

That which we have seen and heard declare we unto you, that ye also may have fellowship with us: and truly our fellowship *is* with the Father, and with his Son Je'-sus [Yeshua] Christ.

And these things write we unto you, that your joy may be full.

1 John 1:1–4

■ *Justice*

Whom God hath set forth *to be* a propitiation through faith in his blood, to declare his righteousness for the remission of sins that are past, through the forbearance of God;

To declare, *I say*, at this time his righteousness: that he might be just, and the justifier of him which believeth in Je'-sus [Yeshua].

Romans 3:25–26

■ *Love*

For I am persuaded, that neither death, nor life, nor angels, nor principalities, nor powers, nor things present, nor things to come,

Nor height, nor depth, nor any other creature, shall be able to separate us from the love of God, which is in Christ Je'-sus [Yeshua] our Lord.

Romans 8:38–39

■ *Peace*

Therefore being justified by faith, we have peace with God through our Lord Je'-sus [Yeshua] Christ:

By whom also we have access by faith into this grace wherein we stand, and rejoice in hope of the glory of God.

Romans 5:1–2

■ *Rescue*

I thank God through Je'-sus [Yeshua] Christ our Lord. So then with the mind I myself serve the law of God; but with the flesh the law of sin.

Romans 7:25

For from you sounded out the word of the Lord not only in Mac-e-do'-ni-a and A-chai'-a, but also in every place your faith to God-ward is spread abroad; so that we need not to speak any thing.

For they themselves shew of us what manner of entering in we had unto you, and how ye turned to God from idols to serve the living and true God;

And to wait for his Son from heaven, whom he raised from the dead, *even* Je'-sus [Yeshua], which delivered us from the wrath to come.

1 Thessalonians 1:8–10

For if after they have escaped the pollutions of the world through the knowledge of the Lord and Saviour Je'-sus [Yeshua] Christ, they are again entangled therein, and overcome, the latter end is worse with them than the beginning.

2 Peter 2:20

▪ *Rest*

Je'-sus [Yeshua] answered and said unto her, Whosoever drinketh of this water shall thirst again.

But whosoever drinketh of the water that I shall give him shall never thirst; but the water that I shall give him shall be in him a well of water springing up into everlasting life.

John 4:13–14

▪ *Strength*

Now to him that is of power to stablish you according to my gospel, and the preaching of Je'-sus [Yeshua] Christ, according to the revelation of the mystery, which was kept secret since the world began,

But now is made manifest, and by the scriptures of the prophets, according to the commandment of the everlasting God, made known to all nations for the obedience of faith.

Romans 16:25–26

Who shall also confirm you unto the end, *that ye may be* blameless in the day of our Lord Je'-sus [Yeshua] Christ.

God *is* faithful, by whom ye were called unto the fellowship of his Son Je'-sus [Yeshua] Christ our Lord.

1 Corinthians 1:8–9

Thou therefore, my son, be strong in the grace that is in Christ Je'-sus [Yeshua].

2 Timothy 2:1

■ *Victory*

So when this corruptible shall have put on incorruption, and this mortal shall have put on immortality, then shall be brought to pass the saying that is written, Death is swallowed up in victory.

O death, where *is* thy sting? O grave, where *is* thy victory?

The sting of death *is* sin; and the strength of sin *is* the law.

But thanks *be* to God, which giveth us the victory through our Lord Je'-sus [Yeshua] Christ.

1 Corinthians 15:54–57

Being confident of this very thing, that he which hath begun a good work in you will perform *it* until the day of Je'-sus [Yeshua] Christ.

Philippians 1:6

Seeing then that we have a great high priest, that is passed into the heavens, Je'-sus [Yeshua] the Son of God, let us hold fast *our* profession.

For we have not an high priest which cannot be touched with the feeling of our infirmities; but was in all points tempted like as *we are*, *yet* without sin.

Let us therefore come boldly unto the throne of grace, that we may obtain mercy, and find grace to help in time of need.

Hebrews 4:14–16

For men verily swear by the greater: and an oath for confirmation *is* to them an end of all strife.

Wherein God, willing more abundantly to shew unto the heirs of promise the immutability of his counsel, confirmed *it* by an oath:

That by two immutable things, in which *it was* impossible for God to lie, we might have a strong consolation, who have fled for refuge to lay hold upon the hope set before us:

Which *hope* we have as an anchor of the soul, both sure and stedfast, and which entereth into that within the veil;

Whither the forerunner is for us entered, *even* Je'-sus [Yeshua], made an high priest for ever after the order of Mel-chis'-e-dec.

Hebrews 6:16–20

God's Promises Help Me Know . . .

■ *The Future*

And Je'-sus [Yeshua] answered and said, Verily I say unto you, There is no man that hath left house, or brethren, or sisters, or father, or mother, or wife, or children, or lands, for my sake, and the gospel's,

But he shall receive an hundredfold now in this time, houses, and brethren, and sisters, and mothers, and children, and lands, with persecutions; and in the world to come eternal life.

But many *that are* first shall be last; and the last first.

Mark 10:29–31

Who shall also confirm you unto the end, *that ye may be* blameless in the day of our Lord Je'-sus [Yeshua] Christ.

God *is* faithful, by whom ye were called unto the fellowship of his Son Je'-sus [Yeshua] Christ our Lord

1 Corinthians 1:8–9

Being confident of this very thing, that he which hath begun a good work in you will perform *it* until the day of Je'-sus [Yeshua] Christ.

Philippians 1:6

Since we heard of your faith in Christ Je'-sus [Yeshua], and of the love *which ye have* to all the saints,

For the hope which is laid up for you in heaven, whereof ye heard before in the word of the truth of the gospel.

Colossians 1:4–5

And Je′-sus [Yeshua] answered and said, Verily I say unto you, There is no man that hath left house, or brethren, or sisters, or father, or mother, or wife, or children, or lands, for my sake, and the gospel's,

But he shall receive an hundredfold now in this time, houses, and brethren, and sisters, and mothers, and children, and lands, with persecutions; and in the world to come eternal life.

But many *that are* first shall be last; and the last first.

Mark 10:29–31

Je′-sus [Yeshua] answered and said unto her, Whosoever drinketh of this water shall thirst again.

But whosoever drinketh of the water that I shall give him shall never thirst; but the water that I shall give him shall be in him a well of water springing up into everlasting life.

John 4:13–14

Je′-sus [Yeshua] said unto her, I am the resurrection, and the life: he that believeth in me, though he were dead, yet shall he live:

And whosoever liveth and believeth in me shall never die. Believest thou this?

John 11:25–26

That as sin hath reigned unto death, even so might grace reign through righteousness unto eternal life by Je'-sus [Yeshua] Christ our Lord.

Romans 5:21

But now being made free from sin, and become servants to God, ye have your fruit unto holiness, and the end everlasting life.

For the wages of sin *is* death; but the gift of God *is* eternal life through Je'-sus [Yeshua] Christ our Lord.

Romans 6:22–23

Even when we were dead in sins, hath quickened us together with Christ, (by grace ye are saved;)

And hath raised *us* up together, and made *us* sit together in heavenly *places* in Christ Je'-sus [Yeshua]:

That in the ages to come he might shew the exceeding riches of his grace in *his* kindness toward us through Christ Je'-sus [Yeshua].

Ephesians 2:5–7

Since we heard of your faith in Christ Je'-sus [Yeshua], and of the love *which ye have* to all the saints,

For the hope which is laid up for you in heaven, whereof ye heard before in the word of the truth of the gospel.

Colossians 1:4–5

Paul, a servant of God, and an apostle of Je'-sus [Yeshua] Christ, according to the faith of God's elect, and the acknowledging of the truth which is after godliness;

In hope of eternal life, which God, that cannot lie, promised before the world began.

Titus 1:1–2

■ Hope for Living

What shall we then say to these things? If God *be* for us, who *can be* against us?

He that spared not his own Son, but delivered him up for us all, how shall he not with him also freely give us all things?

Who shall lay any thing to the charge of God's elect? *It is* God that justifieth.

Who *is* he that condemneth? *It is* Christ that died, yea rather, that is risen again, who is even at the right hand of God, who also maketh intercession for us.

Who shall separate us from the love of Christ? *shall* tribulation, or distress, or persecution, or famine, or nakedness, or peril, or sword?

As it is written, For thy sake we are killed all the day long; we are accounted as sheep for the slaughter.

Nay, in all these things we are more than conquerors through him that loved us.

For I am persuaded, that neither death, nor life, nor angels, nor principalities, nor powers, nor things present, nor things to come,

Nor height, nor depth, nor any other creature, shall be able to separate us from the love of God, which is in Christ Je′-sus [Yeshua] our Lord.

Romans 8:31–39

Being confident of this very thing, that he which hath begun a good work in you will perform *it* until the day of Je'-sus [Yeshua] Christ.

Philippians 1:6

Now our Lord Je'-sus [Yeshua] Christ himself, and God, even our Father, which hath loved us, and hath given *us* everlasting consolation and good hope through grace,

Comfort your hearts, and stablish you in every good word and work.

2 Thessalonians 2:16–17

Hope for the Resurrection

But he held his peace, and answered nothing. Again the high priest asked him, and said unto him, Art thou the Christ, the Son of the Blessed?

And Je'-sus [Yeshua] said, I am: and ye shall see the Son of man sitting on the right hand of power, and coming in the clouds of heaven.

Mark 14:61–62

Behold, I shew you a mystery; We shall not all sleep, but we shall all be changed,

In a moment, in the twinkling of an eye, at the last trump: for the trumpet shall sound, and the dead shall be raised incorruptible, and we shall be changed.

For this corruptible must put on incorruption, and this mortal *must* put on immortality.

So when this corruptible shall have put on incorruption, and this mortal shall have put on immortality, then shall be brought to pass the saying that is written, Death is swallowed up in victory.

O death, where *is* thy sting? O grave, where *is* thy victory?

The sting of death *is* sin; and the strength of sin *is* the law.

But thanks *be* to God, which giveth us the victory through our Lord Je'-sus [Yeshua] Christ.

1 Corinthians 15:51–57

For if we believe that Je'-sus [Yeshua] died and rose again, even so them also which sleep in Je'-sus [Yeshua] will God bring with him.

1 Thessalonians 4:14

For God hath not appointed us to wrath, but to obtain salvation by our Lord Je'-sus [Yeshua] Christ,

Who died for us, that, whether we wake or sleep, we should live together with him.

Wherefore comfort yourselves together, and edify one another, even as also ye do.

1 Thessalonians 5:9–11

Then Pe'-ter said unto them, Repent, and be baptized every one of you in the name of Je'-sus [Yeshua] Christ for the remission of sins, and ye shall receive the gift of the Ho'-ly Ghost.

For the promise is unto you, and to your children, and to all that are afar off, *even* as many as the Lord our God shall call.

Acts 2:38–39

Christ hath redeemed us from the curse of the law, being made a curse for us: for it is written, Cursed *is* every one that hangeth on a tree:

That the blessing of A'-bra-ham might come on the Gen'-tiles through Je'-sus [Yeshua] Christ; that we might receive the promise of the Spir'-it through faith.

Galatians 3:13–14

Now therefore ye are no more strangers and foreigners, but fellowcitizens with the saints, and of the household of God;

And are built upon the foundation of the apostles and prophets, Je'-sus [Yeshua] Christ himself being the chief corner *stone*;

In whom all the building fitly framed together groweth unto an holy temple in the Lord:

In whom ye also are builded together for an habitation of God through the Spir'-it.

Ephesians 2:19–22

◼ The Presence of the Son

And Je'-sus [Yeshua] came and spake unto them, saying, All power is given unto me in heaven and in earth.

Go ye therefore, and teach all nations, baptizing them in the name of the Father, and of the Son, and of the Ho'-ly Ghost:

Teaching them to observe all things whatsoever I have commanded you: and, lo, I am with you alway, *even* unto the end of the world. A'-men.

Matthew 28:18–20

Je'-sus [Yeshua] answered and said unto him, If a man love me, he will keep my words: and my Father will love him, and we will come unto him, and make our abode with him.

John 14:23

◼ The Return of Christ

For our conversation is in heaven; from whence also we look for the Saviour, the Lord Je'-sus [Yeshua] Christ:

Who shall change our vile body, that it may be fashioned like unto his glorious body, according to the working whereby he is able even to subdue all things unto himself.

Philippians 3:20–21

Who shall also confirm you unto the end, *that ye may be* blameless in the day of our Lord Je′-sus [Ye-shua] Christ.

God *is* faithful, by whom ye were called unto the fellowship of his Son Je′-sus [Yeshua] Christ our Lord.

1 Corinthians 1:8–9

And the very God of peace sanctify you wholly; and *I pray God* your whole spirit and soul and body be preserved blameless unto the coming of our Lord Je′-sus [Yeshua] Christ.

Faithful *is* he that calleth you, who also will do *it*.

1 Thessalonians 5:23–24

God Promises Help When I Feel . . .

■ *Anger*

For God hath not appointed us to wrath, but to obtain salvation by our Lord Je′-sus [Yeshua] Christ,

Who died for us, that, whether we wake or sleep, we should live together with him.

Wherefore comfort yourselves together, and edify one another, even as also ye do.

1 Thessalonians 5:9–11

■ *Anxiety*

Rejoice in the Lord alway: *and* again I say, Rejoice.

Let your moderation be known unto all men. The Lord *is* at hand.

Be careful for nothing; but in every thing by prayer and supplication with thanksgiving let your requests be made known unto God.

And the peace of God, which passeth all understanding, shall keep your hearts and minds through Christ Je′-sus [Yeshua].

Philippians 4:4–7

Unto Tim′-o-thy, *my* own son in the faith: Grace, mercy, *and* peace, from God our Father and Je′-sus [Yeshua] Christ our Lord.

1 Timothy 1:2

To Ti′-tus, *mine* own son after the common faith: Grace, mercy, *and* peace, from God the Father and the Lord Je′-sus [Yeshua] Christ our Saviour.

Titus 1:4

■ *Discouragement*

For ye know the grace of our Lord Je′-sus [Yeshua] Christ, that, though he was rich, yet for your sakes he became poor, that ye through his poverty might be rich.

2 Corinthians 8:9

Blessed *be* the God and Father of our Lord Je'-sus [Yeshua] Christ, who hath blessed us with all spiritual blessings in heavenly *places* in Christ.

Ephesians 1:3

◼ *Doubt*

And Je'-sus [Yeshua] answering saith unto them, Have faith in God.

For verily I say unto you, That whosoever shall say unto this mountain, Be thou removed, and be thou cast into the sea; and shall not doubt in his heart, but shall believe that those things which he saith shall come to pass; he shall have whatsoever he saith.

Therefore I say unto you, What things soever ye desire, when ye pray, believe that ye receive *them*, and ye shall have *them*.

Mark 11:22–24

Who shall also confirm you unto the end, *that ye may be* blameless in the day of our Lord Je'-sus [Yeshua] Christ.

God *is* faithful, by whom ye were called unto the fellowship of his Son Je'-sus [Yeshua] Christ our Lord.

1 Corinthians 1:8–9

Being confident of this very thing, that he which hath begun a good work in you will perform *it* until the day of Je'-sus [Yeshua] Christ.

Philippians 1:6

And the very God of peace sanctify you wholly; and
I *pray God* your whole spirit and soul and body be pre-
served blameless unto the coming of our Lord Je'-sus
[Yeshua] Christ.

Faithful *is* he that calleth you, who also will do *it*.

1 Thessalonians 5:23–24

■ *Worry*

Now unto him that is able to do exceeding abundantly
above all that we ask or think, according to the power
that worketh in us,

Unto him *be* glory in the church by Christ Je'-sus [Ye-
shua] throughout all ages, world without end. A'-men.

Ephesians 3:20–21

Rejoice in the Lord alway: *and* again I say, Rejoice.

Let your moderation be known unto all men. The Lord
is at hand.

Be careful for nothing; but in every thing by prayer
and supplication with thanksgiving let your requests be
made known unto God.

And the peace of God, which passeth all understanding, shall keep your hearts and minds through Christ
Je'-sus [Yeshua].

Philippians 4:4–7

God Promises That I Can Stand Against . . .

■ *Death*

But now being made free from sin, and become servants to God, ye have your fruit unto holiness, and the end everlasting life.

For the wages of sin *is* death; but the gift of God *is* eternal life through Je′-sus [Yeshua] Christ our Lord.

Romans 6:22–23

For I am persuaded, that neither death, nor life, nor angels, nor principalities, nor powers, nor things present, nor things to come,

Nor height, nor depth, nor any other creature, shall be able to separate us from the love of God, which is in Christ Je′-sus [Yeshua] our Lord.

Romans 8:38–39

■ *Failure*

But their scribes and Phar′-i-sees murmured against his disciples, saying, Why do ye eat and drink with publicans and sinners?

And Je′-sus [Yeshua] answering said unto them, They that are whole need not a physician; but they that are sick.

Luke 5:30–31

Even when we were dead in sins, hath quickened us together with Christ, (by grace ye are saved;)

And hath raised *us* up together, and made *us* sit together in heavenly *places* in Christ Je′-sus [Yeshua]:

That in the ages to come he might shew the exceeding riches of his grace in *his* kindness toward us through Christ Je′-sus [Yeshua].

Ephesians 2:5–7

This *is* a faithful saying, and worthy of all acceptation, that Christ Je′-sus [Yeshua] came into the world to save sinners; of whom I am chief.

1 Timothy 1:15

Who hath saved us, and called *us* with an holy calling, not according to our works, but according to his own purpose and grace, which was given us in Christ Je′-sus [Yeshua] before the world began.

2 Timothy 1:9

■ *Persecution*

And Je′-sus [Yeshua] answered and said, Verily I say unto you, There is no man that hath left house, or brethren, or sisters, or father, or mother, or wife, or children, or lands, for my sake, and the gospel's,

But he shall receive an hundredfold now in this time, houses, and brethren, and sisters, and mothers, and children, and lands, with persecutions; and in the world to come eternal life.

But many *that are* first shall be last; and the last first.

Mark 10:29–31

What shall we then say to these things? If God *be* for us, who *can be* against us?

He that spared not his own Son, but delivered him up for us all, how shall he not with him also freely give us all things?

Who shall lay any thing to the charge of God's elect? *It is* God that justifieth.

Who *is* he that condemneth? *It is* Christ that died, yea rather, that is risen again, who is even at the right hand of God, who also maketh intercession for us.

Who shall separate us from the love of Christ? *shall* tribulation, or distress, or persecution, or famine, or nakedness, or peril, or sword?

As it is written, For thy sake we are killed all the day long; we are accounted as sheep for the slaughter.

Nay, in all these things we are more than conquerors through him that loved us.

For I am persuaded, that neither death, nor life, nor angels, nor principalities, nor powers, nor things present, nor things to come,

Nor height, nor depth, nor any other creature, shall be able to separate us from the love of God, which is in Christ Je'-sus [Yeshua] our Lord.

Romans 8:31–39

▪ *Rejection*

For if by one man's offence death reigned by one; much more they which receive abundance of grace and of the gift of righteousness shall reign in life by one, Je′-sus [Yeshua] Christ.

Romans 5:17

That as sin hath reigned unto death, even so might grace reign through righteousness unto eternal life by Je′-sus [Yeshua] Christ our Lord.

Romans 5:21

Grace *be* with all them that love our Lord Je′-sus [Yeshua] Christ in sincerity. A′-men.

Ephesians 6:24

Being confident of this very thing, that he which hath begun a good work in you will perform *it* until the day of Je′-sus [Yeshua] Christ.

Philippians 1:6

▪ *Sin*

And as they were eating, Je′-sus [Yeshua] took bread, and blessed *it*, and brake *it*, and gave *it* to the disciples, and said, Take, eat; this is my body.

And he took the cup, and gave thanks, and gave *it* to them, saying, Drink ye all of it;

For this is my blood of the new testament, which is shed for many for the remission of sins.

Matthew 26:26–28

Then Pe'-ter said unto them, Repent, and be baptized every one of you in the name of Je'-sus [Yeshua] Christ for the remission of sins, and ye shall receive the gift of the Ho'-ly Ghost.

For the promise is unto you, and to your children, and to all that are afar off, *even* as many as the Lord our God shall call.

Acts 2:38–39

Even the righteousness of God *which is* by faith of Je'-sus [Yeshua] Christ unto all and upon all them that believe: for there is no difference:

For all have sinned, and come short of the glory of God;

Being justified freely by his grace through the redemption that is in Christ Je'-sus [Yeshua]:

Whom God hath set forth *to be* a propitiation through faith in his blood, to declare his righteousness for the remission of sins that are past, through the forbearance of God;

To declare, *I say*, at this time his righteousness: that he might be just, and the justifier of him which believeth in Je'-sus [Yeshua].

Romans 3:22–26

That as sin hath reigned unto death, even so might grace reign through righteousness unto eternal life by Je'-sus [Yeshua] Christ our Lord.

Romans 5:21

Likewise reckon ye also yourselves to be dead indeed unto sin, but alive unto God through Je'-sus [Yeshua] Christ our Lord.

Romans 6:11

But now being made free from sin, and become servants to God, ye have your fruit unto holiness, and the end everlasting life.

For the wages of sin *is* death; but the gift of God *is* eternal life through Je'-sus [Yeshua] Christ our Lord.

Romans 6:22–23

I thank God through Je'-sus [Yeshua] Christ our Lord. So then with the mind I myself serve the law of God; but with the flesh the law of sin.

Romans 7:25

There is therefore now no condemnation to them which are in Christ Je'-sus [Yeshua], who walk not after the flesh, but after the Spir'-it.

For the law of the Spir'-it of life in Christ Je'-sus [Yeshua] hath made me free from the law of sin and death.

Romans 8:1–2

The sting of death *is* sin; and the strength of sin *is* the law.

But thanks *be* to God, which giveth us the victory through our Lord Je'-sus [Yeshua] Christ.

1 Corinthians 15:56–57

But the scripture hath concluded all under sin, that the promise by faith of Je'-sus [Yeshua] Christ might be given to them that believe.

Galatians 3:22

Even when we were dead in sins, hath quickened us together with Christ, (by grace ye are saved;)

And hath raised *us* up together, and made *us* sit together in heavenly *places* in Christ Je'-sus [Yeshua]:

That in the ages to come he might shew the exceeding riches of his grace in *his* kindness toward us through Christ Je'-sus [Yeshua].

Ephesians 2:5–7

But if we walk in the light, as he is in the light, we have fellowship one with another, and the blood of Je'-sus [Yeshua] Christ his Son cleanseth us from all sin.

1 John 1:7

My little children, these things write I unto you, that ye sin not. And if any man sin, we have an advocate with the Father, Je'-sus [Yeshua] Christ the righteous:

And he is the propitiation for our sins: and not for ours only, but also for *the sins of* the whole world.

1 John 2:1–2

■ *Suffering*

Blessed *be* God, even the Father of our Lord Je′-sus [Yeshua] Christ, the Father of mercies, and the God of all comfort;

Who comforteth us in all our tribulation, that we may be able to comfort them which are in any trouble, by the comfort wherewith we ourselves are comforted of God.

For as the sufferings of Christ abound in us, so our consolation also aboundeth by Christ.

2 Corinthians 1:3–5

Be sober, be vigilant; because your adversary the devil, as a roaring lion, walketh about, seeking whom he may devour:

Whom resist stedfast in the faith, knowing that the same afflictions are accomplished in your brethren that are in the world.

But the God of all grace, who hath called us unto his eternal glory by Christ Je′-sus [Yeshua], after that ye have suffered a while, make you perfect, stablish, strengthen, settle *you*.

1 Peter 5:8–10

■ *Temptation*

I thank God through Je′-sus [Yeshua] Christ our Lord. So then with the mind I myself serve the law of God; but with the flesh the law of sin.

Romans 7:25

Seeing then that we have a great high priest, that is passed into the heavens, Je'-sus [Yeshua] the Son of God, let us hold fast *our* profession.

For we have not an high priest which cannot be touched with the feeling of our infirmities; but was in all points tempted like as *we are*, *yet* without sin.

Let us therefore come boldly unto the throne of grace, that we may obtain mercy, and find grace to help in time of need.

Hebrews 4:14–16

For if after they have escaped the pollutions of the world through the knowledge of the Lord and Saviour Je'-sus [Yeshua] Christ, they are again entangled therein, and overcome, the latter end is worse with them than the beginning.

2 Peter 2:20

Through God's Promises I Experience . . .

▪ *Eternal Life*

And Je'-sus [Yeshua] answered and said, Verily I say unto you, There is no man that hath left house, or brethren, or sisters, or father, or mother, or wife, or children, or lands, for my sake, and the gospel's,

But he shall receive an hundredfold now in this time, houses, and brethren, and sisters, and mothers, and children, and lands, with persecutions; and in the world to come eternal life.

But many *that are* first shall be last; and the last first.

Mark 10:29–31

■ *Gifts from God*

Therefore being justified by faith, we have peace with God through our Lord Je'-sus [Yeshua] Christ:

By whom also we have access by faith into this grace wherein we stand, and rejoice in hope of the glory of God.

Romans 5:1–2

Likewise reckon ye also yourselves to be dead indeed unto sin, but alive unto God through Je'-sus [Yeshua] Christ our Lord.

Romans 6:11

But now being made free from sin, and become servants to God, ye have your fruit unto holiness, and the end everlasting life.

For the wages of sin *is* death; but the gift of God *is* eternal life through Je'-sus [Yeshua] Christ our Lord.

Romans 6:22–23

There is therefore now no condemnation to them which are in Christ Je'-sus [Yeshua], who walk not after the flesh, but after the Spir'-it.

For the law of the Spir'-it of life in Christ Je'-sus [Ye-shua] hath made me free from the law of sin and death.

Romans 8:1–2

Who shall also confirm you unto the end, *that ye may be* blameless in the day of our Lord Je'-sus [Ye-shua] Christ.

God *is* faithful, by whom ye were called unto the fellowship of his Son Je'-sus [Yeshua] Christ our Lord.

1 Corinthians 1:8–9

Therefore if any man *be* in Christ, *he is* a new creature: old things are passed away; behold, all things are become new.

And all things *are* of God, who hath reconciled us to himself by Je'-sus [Yeshua] Christ, and hath given to us the ministry of reconciliation.

2 Corinthians 5:17–18

For ye know the grace of our Lord Je'-sus [Yeshua] Christ, that, though he was rich, yet for your sakes he became poor, that ye through his poverty might be rich.

2 Corinthians 8:9

Blessed *be* the God and Father of our Lord Je'-sus [Yeshua] Christ, who hath blessed us with all spiritual blessings in heavenly *places* in Christ.

Ephesians 1:3

For we are his workmanship, created in Christ Je′-sus [Yeshua] unto good works, which God hath before ordained that we should walk in them.

Ephesians 2:10

And the very God of peace sanctify you wholly; and *I pray God* your whole spirit and soul and body be preserved blameless unto the coming of our Lord Je′-sus [Yeshua] Christ.

Faithful *is* he that calleth you, who also will do *it*.

1 Thessalonians 5:23–24

But we are bound to give thanks alway to God for you, brethren beloved of the Lord, because God hath from the beginning chosen you to salvation through sanctification of the Spir′-it and belief of the truth:

Whereunto he called you by our gospel, to the obtaining of the glory of our Lord Je′-sus [Yeshua] Christ.

2 Thessalonians 2:13–14

■ *The Mercy of the Father*

Then Pe′-ter said unto them, Repent, and be baptized every one of you in the name of Je′-sus [Yeshua] Christ for the remission of sins, and ye shall receive the gift of the Ho′-ly Ghost.

For the promise is unto you, and to your children, and to all that are afar off, *even* as many as the Lord our God shall call.

Acts 2:38–39

But now the righteousness of God without the law is manifested, being witnessed by the law and the prophets;

Even the righteousness of God *which is* by faith of Je'-sus [Yeshua] Christ unto all and upon all them that believe: for there is no difference.

Romans 3:21–22

For if by one man's offence death reigned by one; much more they which receive abundance of grace and of the gift of righteousness shall reign in life by one, Je'-sus [Yeshua] Christ.

Romans 5:17

Even when we were dead in sins, hath quickened us together with Christ, (by grace ye are saved;)

And hath raised *us* up together, and made *us* sit together in heavenly *places* in Christ Je'-sus [Yeshua]:

That in the ages to come he might shew the exceeding riches of his grace in *his* kindness toward us through Christ Je'-sus [Yeshua].

For by grace are ye saved through faith; and that not of yourselves: *it is* the gift of God:

Not of works, lest any man should boast.

Ephesians 2:5–9

Unto Tim'-o-thy, *my* own son in the faith: Grace, mercy, *and* peace, from God our Father and Je'-sus [Yeshua] Christ our Lord.

1 Timothy 1:2

Who hath saved us, and called *us* with an holy calling, not according to our works, but according to his own purpose and grace, which was given us in Christ Je′-sus [Yeshua] before the world began.

2 Timothy 1:9

■ *The Mercy of the Son*

And as they were eating, Je′-sus [Yeshua] took bread, and blessed *it*, and brake *it*, and gave *it* to the disciples, and said, Take, eat; this is my body.

And he took the cup, and gave thanks, and gave *it* to them, saying, Drink ye all of it;

For this is my blood of the new testament, which is shed for many for the remission of sins.

Matthew 26:26–28

But their scribes and Phar′-i-sees murmured against his disciples, saying, Why do ye eat and drink with publicans and sinners?

And Je′-sus [Yeshua] answering said unto them, They that are whole need not a physician; but they that are sick.

Luke 5:30–31

Even the righteousness of God *which is* by faith of Je′-sus [Yeshua] Christ unto all and upon all them that believe: for there is no difference:

For all have sinned, and come short of the glory of God;

Being justified freely by his grace through the redemption that is in Christ Je'-sus [Yeshua]:

Whom God hath set forth *to be* a propitiation through faith in his blood, to declare his righteousness for the remission of sins that are past, through the forbearance of God;

To declare, *I say*, at this time his righteousness: that he might be just, and the justifier of him which believeth in Je'-sus [Yeshua].

Romans 3:22–26

This *is* a faithful saying, and worthy of all acceptation, that Christ Je'-sus [Yeshua] came into the world to save sinners; of whom I am chief.

1 Timothy 1:15

▓ *Miracles*

Je'-sus [Yeshua] said unto him, If thou canst believe, all things *are* possible to him that believeth.

Mark 9:23

And Je'-sus [Yeshua] answering saith unto them, Have faith in God.

For verily I say unto you, That whosoever shall say unto this mountain, Be thou removed, and be thou cast into the sea; and shall not doubt in his heart, but shall believe that those things which he saith shall come to pass; he shall have whatsoever he saith.

Therefore I say unto you, What things soever ye desire, when ye pray, believe that ye receive *them*, and ye shall have *them*.

Mark 11:22–24

God's Promises Enable My . . .

■ *Belief*

Je′-sus [Yeshua] said unto him, If thou canst believe, all things *are* possible to him that believeth.

Mark 9:23

And Je′-sus [Yeshua] answering saith unto them, Have faith in God.

For verily I say unto you, That whosoever shall say unto this mountain, Be thou removed, and be thou cast into the sea; and shall not doubt in his heart, but shall believe that those things which he saith shall come to pass; he shall have whatsoever he saith.

Therefore I say unto you, What things soever ye desire, when ye pray, believe that ye receive *them*, and ye shall have *them*.

Mark 11:22–24

Then said Je′-sus [Yeshua] to those Jews which believed on him, If ye continue in my word, *then* are ye my disciples indeed;

And ye shall know the truth, and the truth shall make you free.

John 8:31–32

There is therefore now no condemnation to them which are in Christ Je′-sus [Yeshua], who walk not after the flesh, but after the Spir′-it.

For the law of the Spir′-it of life in Christ Je′-sus [Yeshua] hath made me free from the law of sin and death.

Romans 8:1–2

Therefore if any man *be* in Christ, *he is* a new creature: old things are passed away; behold, all things are become new.

And all things *are* of God, who hath reconciled us to himself by Je′-sus [Yeshua] Christ, and hath given to us the ministry of reconciliation.

2 Corinthians 5:17–18

▪ *Faith*

But now the righteousness of God without the law is manifested, being witnessed by the law and the prophets;

Even the righteousness of God *which is* by faith of Je′-sus [Yeshua] Christ unto all and upon all them that believe: for there is no difference:

For all have sinned, and come short of the glory of God;

Being justified freely by his grace through the redemption that is in Christ Je′-sus [Yeshua]:

Whom God hath set forth *to be* a propitiation through faith in his blood, to declare his righteousness for the remission of sins that are past, through the forbearance of God;

To declare, *I say*, at this time his righteousness: that he might be just, and the justifier of him which believeth in Je'-sus [Yeshua].

Romans 3:21–26

Now it was not written for his sake alone, that it was imputed to him;

But for us also, to whom it shall be imputed, if we believe on him that raised up Je'-sus [Yeshua] our Lord from the dead;

Who was delivered for our offences, and was raised again for our justification.

Romans 4:23–25

But what things were gain to me, those I counted loss for Christ.

Yea doubtless, and I count all things *but* loss for the excellency of the knowledge of Christ Je'-sus [Yeshua] my Lord: for whom I have suffered the loss of all things, and do count them *but* dung, that I may win Christ,

And be found in him, not having mine own righteousness, which is of the law, but that which is through the faith of Christ, the righteousness which is of God by faith:

That I may know him, and the power of his resurrection, and the fellowship of his sufferings, being made conformable unto his death;

If by any means I might attain unto the resurrection of the dead.

Philippians 3:7–11

Je′-sus [Yeshua] Christ the same yesterday, and to day, and for ever.

Hebrews 13:8

And we have seen and do testify that the Father sent the Son *to be* the Saviour of the world.

Whosoever shall confess that Je′-sus [Yeshua] is the Son of God, God dwelleth in him, and he in God.

1 John 4:14–15

■ *Obedience*

Je′-sus [Yeshua] answered and said unto him, If a man love me, he will keep my words: and my Father will love him, and we will come unto him, and make our abode with him.

John 14:23

For this is the love of God, that we keep his commandments: and his commandments are not grievous.

For whatsoever is born of God overcometh the world: and this is the victory that overcometh the world, *even* our faith.

Who is he that overcometh the world, but he that believeth that Je′-sus [Yeshua] is the Son of God?

1 John 5:3–5

■ Patience

Whom God hath set forth *to be* a propitiation through faith in his blood, to declare his righteousness for the remission of sins that are past, through the forbearance of God;

To declare, *I say*, at this time his righteousness: that he might be just, and the justifier of him which believeth in Je'-sus [Yeshua].

Romans 3:25–26

■ Perspective of God's Kingdom

And Je'-sus [Yeshua] answered and said, Verily I say unto you, There is no man that hath left house, or brethren, or sisters, or father, or mother, or wife, or children, or lands, for my sake, and the gospel's,

But he shall receive an hundredfold now in this time, houses, and brethren, and sisters, and mothers, and children, and lands, with persecutions; and in the world to come eternal life.

But many *that are* first shall be last; and the last first.

Mark 10:29–31

Now therefore ye are no more strangers and foreigners, but fellowcitizens with the saints, and of the household of God;

And are built upon the foundation of the apostles and prophets, Je'-sus [Yeshua] Christ himself being the chief corner *stone*;

In whom all the building fitly framed together groweth unto an holy temple in the Lord:

In whom ye also are builded together for an habitation of God through the Spir'-it.

Ephesians 2:19–22

By the which will we are sanctified through the offering of the body of Je'-sus [Yeshua] Christ once *for all*.

Hebrews 10:10

▓ *Repentance*

But their scribes and Phar'-i-sees murmured against his disciples, saying, Why do ye eat and drink with publicans and sinners?

And Je'-sus [Yeshua] answering said unto them, They that are whole need not a physician; but they that are sick.

Luke 5:30–31

Then Pe'-ter said unto them, Repent, and be baptized every one of you in the name of Je'-sus [Yeshua] Christ for the remission of sins, and ye shall receive the gift of the Ho'-ly Ghost.

For the promise is unto you, and to your children, and to all that are afar off, *even* as many as the Lord our God shall call.

Acts 2:38–39

Likewise reckon ye also yourselves to be dead indeed unto sin, but alive unto God through Je'-sus [Yeshua] Christ our Lord.

Romans 6:11

But now being made free from sin, and become servants to God, ye have your fruit unto holiness, and the end everlasting life.

For the wages of sin *is* death; but the gift of God *is* eternal life through Je'-sus [Yeshua] Christ our Lord.

Romans 6:22–23

There is therefore now no condemnation to them which are in Christ Je'-sus [Yeshua], who walk not after the flesh, but after the Spir'-it.

For the law of the Spir'-it of life in Christ Je'-sus [Yeshua] hath made me free from the law of sin and death.

Romans 8:1–2

Therefore if any man *be* in Christ, *he is* a new creature: old things are passed away; behold, all things are become new.

And all things *are* of God, who hath reconciled us to himself by Je'-sus [Yeshua] Christ, and hath given to us the ministry of reconciliation;

2 Corinthians 5:17–18

God's Promises Guide Me In . . .

■ *Change*

But their scribes and Phar'-i-sees murmured against his disciples, saying, Why do ye eat and drink with publicans and sinners?

And Je'-sus [Yeshua] answering said unto them, They that are whole need not a physician; but they that are sick.

Luke 5:30–31

Then Pe'-ter said unto them, Repent, and be baptized every one of you in the name of Je'-sus [Yeshua] Christ for the remission of sins, and ye shall receive the gift of the Ho'-ly Ghost.

For the promise is unto you, and to your children, and to all that are afar off, *even* as many as the Lord our God shall call.

Acts 2:38–39

Behold, I shew you a mystery; We shall not all sleep, but we shall all be changed,

In a moment, in the twinkling of an eye, at the last trump: for the trumpet shall sound, and the dead shall be raised incorruptible, and we shall be changed.

For this corruptible must put on incorruption, and this mortal *must* put on immortality.

So when this corruptible shall have put on incorruption, and this mortal shall have put on immortality, then shall be brought to pass the saying that is written, Death is swallowed up in victory.

O death, where *is* thy sting? O grave, where *is* thy victory?

The sting of death *is* sin; and the strength of sin *is* the law.

But thanks *be* to God, which giveth us the victory through our Lord Je'-sus [Yeshua] Christ.

1 Corinthians 15:51–57

For our conversation is in heaven; from whence also we look for the Saviour, the Lord Je'-sus [Yeshua] Christ:

Who shall change our vile body, that it may be fashioned like unto his glorious body, according to the working whereby he is able even to subdue all things unto himself.

Philippians 3:20–21

For men verily swear by the greater: and an oath for confirmation *is* to them an end of all strife.

Wherein God, willing more abundantly to shew unto the heirs of promise the immutability of his counsel, confirmed *it* by an oath:

That by two immutable things, in which *it was* impossible for God to lie, we might have a strong consolation, who have fled for refuge to lay hold upon the hope set before us:

Which *hope* we have as an anchor of the soul, both sure and stedfast, and which entereth into that within the veil;

Whither the forerunner is for us entered, *even* Je'-sus [Yeshua], made an high priest for ever after the order of Mel-chis'-e-dec.

Hebrews 6:16–20

■ *Fruitfulness*

Being filled with the fruits of righteousness, which are by Je'-sus [Yeshua] Christ, unto the glory and praise of God.

Philippians 1:11

■ *Money*

But my God shall supply all your need according to his riches in glory by Christ Je'-sus [Yeshua].

Now unto God and our Father *be* glory for ever and ever. A'-men.

Philippians 4:19–20

■ *Prayer*

Je'-sus [Yeshua] said unto him, If thou canst believe, all things *are* possible to him that believeth.

Mark 9:23

And Je'-sus [Yeshua] answering saith unto them, Have faith in God.

For verily I say unto you, That whosoever shall say unto this mountain, Be thou removed, and be thou cast into the sea; and shall not doubt in his heart, but shall believe that those things which he saith shall come to pass; he shall have whatsoever he saith.

Therefore I say unto you, What things soever ye desire, when ye pray, believe that ye receive *them*, and ye shall have *them*.

Mark 11:22–24

Therefore being justified by faith, we have peace with God through our Lord Je'-sus [Yeshua] Christ:

By whom also we have access by faith into this grace wherein we stand, and rejoice in hope of the glory of God.

Romans 5:1–2

Rejoice in the Lord alway: *and* again I say, Rejoice.

Let your moderation be known unto all men. The Lord *is* at hand.

Be careful for nothing; but in every thing by prayer and supplication with thanksgiving let your requests be made known unto God.

And the peace of God, which passeth all understanding, shall keep your hearts and minds through Christ Je'-sus [Yeshua].

Philippians 4:4–7

My little children, these things write I unto you, that ye sin not. And if any man sin, we have an advocate with the Father, Je'-sus [Yeshua] Christ the righteous:

And he is the propitiation for our sins: and not for ours only, but also for *the sins of* the whole world.

1 John 2:1–2

■ *Relationships*

And the Lord make you to increase and abound in love one toward another, and toward all *men*, even as we *do* toward you:

To the end he may stablish your hearts unblameable in holiness before God, even our Father, at the coming of our Lord Je′-sus [Yeshua] Christ with all his saints.

1 Thessalonians 3:12–13

But if we walk in the light, as he is in the light, we have fellowship one with another, and the blood of Je′-sus [Yeshua] Christ his Son cleanseth us from all sin.

1 John 1:7

■ *Responsibility*

Who shall also confirm you unto the end, *that ye may be* blameless in the day of our Lord Je′-sus [Yeshua] Christ.

God *is* faithful, by whom ye were called unto the fellowship of his Son Je′-sus [Yeshua] Christ our Lord.

1 Corinthians 1:8–9

Being filled with the fruits of righteousness, which are by Je′-sus [Yeshua] Christ, unto the glory and praise of God.

Philippians 1:11

And *that* every tongue should confess that Je′-sus [Yeshua] Christ *is* Lord, to the glory of God the Father.

Wherefore, my beloved, as ye have always obeyed, not as in my presence only, but now much more in my absence, work out your own salvation with fear and trembling.

Philippians 2:11–12

Be sober, be vigilant; because your adversary the devil, as a roaring lion, walketh about, seeking whom he may devour:

Whom resist stedfast in the faith, knowing that the same afflictions are accomplished in your brethren that are in the world.

But the God of all grace, who hath called us unto his eternal glory by Christ Je′-sus [Yeshua], after that ye have suffered a while, make you perfect, stablish, strengthen, settle *you*.

1 Peter 5:8–10

▪ Work

For we are his workmanship, created in Christ Je′-sus [Yeshua] unto good works, which God hath before or-dained that we should walk in them.

Ephesians 2:10

Being confident of this very thing, that he which hath begun a good work in you will perform *it* until the day of Je′-sus [Yeshua] Christ.

Philippians 1:6

■ *Worship*

Then Pe'-ter said unto them, Repent, and be baptized every one of you in the name of Je'-sus [Yeshua] Christ for the remission of sins, and ye shall receive the gift of the Ho'-ly Ghost.

For the promise is unto you, and to your children, and to all that are afar off, *even* as many as the Lord our God shall call.

Acts 2:38–39

Blessed *be* the God and Father of our Lord Je'-sus [Yeshua] Christ, who hath blessed us with all spiritual blessings in heavenly *places* in Christ.

Ephesians 1:3

Being filled with the fruits of righteousness, which are by Je'-sus [Yeshua] Christ, unto the glory and praise of God.

Philippians 1:11

Rejoice in the Lord alway: *and* again I say, Rejoice.

Let your moderation be known unto all men. The Lord *is* at hand.

Be careful for nothing; but in every thing by prayer and supplication with thanksgiving let your requests be made known unto God.

And the peace of God, which passeth all understanding, shall keep your hearts and minds through Christ Je'-sus [Yeshua].

Philippians 4:4–7

As ye have therefore received Christ Je'-sus [Yeshua] the Lord, *so* walk ye in him:

Rooted and built up in him, and stablished in the faith, as ye have been taught, abounding therein with thanksgiving.

Colossians 2:6–7

But we are bound to give thanks alway to God for you, brethren beloved of the Lord, because God hath from the beginning chosen you to salvation through sanctification of the Spir'-it and belief of the truth:

Whereunto he called you by our gospel, to the obtaining of the glory of our Lord Je'-sus [Yeshua] Christ.

2 Thessalonians 2:13–14

Knowing God's Promises

A Plan of Salvation

Jesus said, "I am the resurrection, and the life: he that believeth in me, though he were dead, yet shall he live: And whosoever liveth and believeth in me shall never die. Believest thou this?" (John 11:25–26).

What must you believe concerning this source of life in order to have it? The Bible's answer is that first you must face the evil that you have done and admit that you cannot be God's unless Jesus takes away your dirtiness and makes you acceptable.

God cannot have evil in his majestic presence, and we all do the things he forbids. The book of Romans tells us, "Even the righteousness of God which is by faith of Jesus Christ unto all and upon all them that believe: for there is no difference: For all have sinned, and come short of the glory of God" (3:22–23). We fall short of whatever moral standards we set for ourselves, let alone the standards set by a Creator who is perfect and holy. Without an answer to sin, none of us can escape the judgment that God has also promised.

Our hopeless plight changed dramatically when Jesus Christ, "God with us," took personal sins vicariously on himself and accepted God's judgment. Jesus fulfilled God's promises by accepting God's rejection and death although he was without sin.

Romans 5:21 makes this promise that explains what happened: "That as sin hath reigned unto death, even so might grace reign through righteousness unto eternal life by Je'-sus [Yeshua] Christ our Lord."

After we admit our need, the second action we must take is to believe that Jesus is the one he said he was and accept him as our ruler, our Lord. When one man asked how to be saved, he heard the wonderful promise, "Believe on the Lord Je'-sus [Yeshua] Christ, and thou shalt be saved, and thy house" (Acts 16:31).

There is nothing else that anyone can do to be accepted by God. Jesus said, "I am the way, the truth, and the life: no man cometh unto the Father, but by me" (John 14:6).

Once we believe, turning over our life to Jesus, we can hear a great promise from Romans 5:1–2: "Therefore being justified by faith, we have peace with God through our Lord Je'-sus [Yeshua] Christ: By whom also we have access by faith into this grace wherein we stand, and rejoice in hope of the glory of God."

GET TO KNOW GOD
On a Deeper Level by Discovering His Biblical Names and Titles

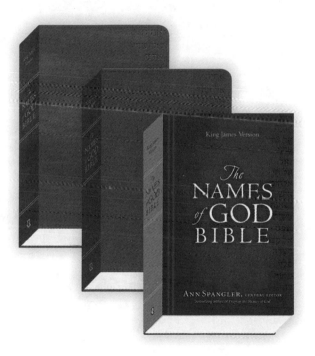